Building a Career in Opera from School to Stage

Building a Career in Opera from School to Stage: Operapreneurship provides early-career singers with an overview of the structure of the opera industry and tools for strategically approaching a career within it. Today's voice students leave the conservatory with better training than ever, but often face challenges to managing their own careers after graduation. This book addresses what singers need to know in order to craft a career path in the contemporary landscape of opera.

Readers learn about the opera industry's structure, common pathways and entry points, non-academic training programs, researching and evaluating opportunities, crafting professional documents and media, and what it means to be a professional opera singer. Written by a singer with recent experience in the industry—and particularly the emerging phase—this book is a practical guide for all singers embarking on a career in opera.

The author's website, www.OperaCareers.com, hosts additional resources including databases of training programs, guides and templates for creating professional documents, as well as articles addressing current industry issues and interviews with subject matter experts.

James Harrington is a professional operatic bass and Paul J. Collins Wisconsin Distinguished Fellow at the Mead Witter School of Music at the University of Wisconsin–Madison. A graduate of Berklee College of Music, he worked for several years in the music industry before deciding to train as an opera singer. He holds the Master of Music in voice performance from Florida State University and is pursuing the Doctor of Musical Arts in voice at the University of Wisconsin. As a singer, he has appeared with the Santa Fe Opera, Portland Opera, Nashville Opera, Teatro Nuovo, Sarasota Opera, and Opera Idaho, among others.

CMS Emerging Fields in Music
Series Editor: *Mark Rabideau, DePauw University, USA*
Managing Editor: *Zoua Sylvia Yang, DePauw University, USA*

The *CMS Series in Emerging Fields in Music* consists of concise monographs that help the profession re-imagine how we must prepare 21st Century Musicians. Shifting cultural landscapes, emerging technologies, and a changing profession in-and-out of the academy demand that we re-examine our relationships with audiences, leverage our art to strengthen the communities in which we live and work, equip our students to think and act as artist-entrepreneurs, explore the limitless (and sometimes limiting) role technology plays in the life of a musician, revisit our very assumptions about what artistic excellence means and how personal creativity must be repositioned at the center of this definition, and share best practices and our own stories of successes and failures when leading institutional change.

These short-form books can be either single-authored works, or contributed volumes comprised of three or four essays on related topics. The books should prove useful for emerging musicians inventing the future they hope to inhabit, faculty rethinking the courses they teach and how they teach them, and administrators guiding curricular innovation and rebranding institutional identity.

Identity and Diversity in New Music
The New Complexities
Marilyn Nonken

Beyond the Conservatory Model
Reimagining Classical Music Performance Training in Higher Education
Michael Stepniak with Peter Sirotin

Building a Career in Opera from School to Stage
Operapreneurship
James Harrington

For more information, please visit: www.routledge.com/CMS-Emerging-Fields-in-Music/book-series/CMSEMR

Building a Career in Opera from School to Stage
Operapreneurship

James Harrington

NEW YORK AND LONDON

First published 2020
by Routledge
52 Vanderbilt Avenue, New York, NY 10017

and by Routledge
2 Park Square, Milton Park, Abingdon, Oxon, OX14 4RN

Routledge is an imprint of the Taylor & Francis Group, an informa business

© 2020 Taylor & Francis

The right of James Harrington to be identified as author of this work has been asserted by him in accordance with sections 77 and 78 of the Copyright, Designs and Patents Act 1988.

All rights reserved. No part of this book may be reprinted or reproduced or utilised in any form or by any electronic, mechanical, or other means, now known or hereafter invented, including photocopying and recording, or in any information storage or retrieval system, without permission in writing from the publishers.

Trademark notice: Product or corporate names may be trademarks or registered trademarks, and are used only for identification and explanation without intent to infringe.

Library of Congress Cataloging-in-Publication Data
Names: Harrington, James (Bass) author.
Title: Building a career in opera from school to stage: operapreneurship / James Harrington.
Description: [1.] | New York: Routledge, 2020. |
Series: CMS emerging fields in music |
Includes bibliographical references and index.
Identifiers: LCCN 2020006051 (print) | LCCN 2020006052 (ebook) | ISBN 9780367421519 (hardback) | ISBN 9780367822224 (ebook)
Subjects: LCSH: Opera–Vocational guidance. |
Singing–Vocational guidance.
Classification: LCC ML3795 .H3307 2020 (print) |
LCC ML3795 (ebook) | DDC 782.1023–dc23
LC record available at https://lccn.loc.gov/2020006051
LC ebook record available at https://lccn.loc.gov/2020006052

ISBN: 978-0-367-42151-9 (hbk)
ISBN: 978-0-367-82222-4 (ebk)

Typeset in Sabon
by Newgen Publishing UK

To Marah
who has dreamt with me,
sacrificed incalculably,
and through her faith
made everything possible.

Contents

Series Editor's Introduction	ix
List of Figures	x
List of Tables	xi
Acknowledgements	xii
Introduction	1

PART I
The Industry from 30,000 Feet ... 7

1 Opera Companies ... 9

2 Other Performing Arts Organizations ... 16

3 Management ... 23

PART II
How a Young Singer Prepares ... 33

4 Formal Training ... 35

5 Non-Academic Training Programs: PTSs, YAPs, and RAPs ... 45

6 Your Team ... 57

7 Research ... 63

PART III
The Nuts and Bolts of Booking Work   75

8   Professional Documents   77

9   Cultivating Your Online Presence   90

10   You, Inc. (Building Your Business)   99

11   Auditions, Rep Books, and Pianists   115

12   Beyond #bookedandblessed: Working in an Opera House   132

Epilogue: The Best of All Possible Careers   144

Glossary   147
Index   152

Series Editor's Introduction

Music is embraced throughout every culture without boundaries. Today, an increasingly connected world offers influence and inspiration for opening our imaginations, as technology provides unprecedented access to global audiences. Communities gather around music to mourn collective hardships and celebrate shared moments, and every parent understands that music enhances their child's chances to succeed in life. Yet it has never been more of a struggle for musicians to make a living at their art—at least when following traditional paths.

The College Music Society's *Emerging Fields in Music Series* champions the search for solutions to the most pressing challenges and most influential opportunities presented to the music profession during this time of uncertainty and promise. This series re-examines how we as music professionals can build relationships with audiences, leverage our art to strengthen the communities in which we live and work, equip our students to think and act as artist-entrepreneurs, explore the limitless (and sometimes limiting) role technology plays in the creation and dissemination of music, revisit our very assumptions about what artistic excellence means, and share best practices and our own stories of successes and failures when leading institutional change.

These short-form books are written for emerging musicians busy inventing the future they hope to inherit, faculty rethinking the courses they teach (curriculum) and how they teach them (pedagogy), and administrators rebranding institutional identity and reshaping the student experience.

The world (and the profession) is changing. And so must we, if we are to carry forward our most beloved traditions of the past and create an audience for our best future.

Mark Rabideau

Figures

4.1 The Opera Career Roadmap   36
4.2 The Opera Career Breakdown   37

Tables

1.1	Opera America Budget Levels	10
5.1	Tiered YAPs	49
10.1	Simple Monthly Budget	100
10.2	Chronological Budget	101
10.3	Deductible Expenses	102
10.4	Sample Travel Log	105
10.5	Legal Structure of Business	107
12.1	Tracking Holloway's "Rule of 25s," each "X" represents 25 perfect repetitions	133

Acknowledgements

Like everyone who undertakes this sort of project, in the course of writing this book I came to the humbling realization of how many people contribute to a project of this scope in ways visible and invisible. As I started to pull the thread of my gratitude and untangle the pile of my influences, I was reminded of what a profoundly charmed life I have had, to be blessed—through no merit of my own—with such generous, brilliant, and loving people at every turn. Some of their contributions have accompanying citations in the text; others have their work cited here, with my undying gratitude. This book exists because of ...

... my family, who raised, nurtured, taught, and loved me. My wife, Marah, whose fingerprints are in so many places in this book that she should have co-author credit. My parents, John and Kyriaki Harrington—the former of whom gave me my love of music and the latter my love of the written word. Mary Harrington Johnson, who is the best friend and sister a human could ever have—one of the greatest graces in my life was having you beside me to lift me up through the darkest point in it. I will never be able to thank you sufficiently for all the things you have always been to me so effortlessly. My wonderful in-laws, Reiner and Madelon Kirsten, who have been an invaluable support system for the last ten years, and are, in large part, the reason this book was conceived. Amy and Gabe Francisco, who took me in during a very cold few weeks in January while I began to rewrite this manuscript. And John and Michelle Thompson, who have been family since the day we met, and who have given of themselves their whole lives in the most beautiful of ways. Thank you for being my family when I first came to Nashville and ever since.

... the many subject matter experts who lent me their thoughts so generously, and without whom this would just be a book full of my opinions. They include Emily Ruth Allen, Dr. Alain Barker, Terrence Chin-Loy, Rebecca Pyle Davis, Dr. Kristina Driskill, Matthew Epstein,

David Salsbery Fry, Dr. Barrett Hipes, Mary Javian, Jeremiah Johnson, Michelle Johnson, Jonathan Kuuskoski, Will Liverman, Dr. William Lumpkin, Joshua Major, Melinda Massie, Lucas Meachem, Dr. Justin John Moniz, Stanford Olsen, Rachel Roberts, Morris Robinson, Reggie Smith, Jr., and Kristin Suess.

... people who, at some point, believed in my abilities and/or inspired me to go forward in this career: Michael Ballam, Townsend Belisle, Samrat Chakrabarti, Keith Chambers, Kathleen Clawson, Doug Han, David Holloway, John Hoomes, Gayletha Nichols, Philip Pierce, Richard Russell, Matthew Treviño, Robert Tweten, Amy Tate Williams, and Justin Werner.

... several people who lent a platform or support to this material in its nascent phase, for which I am most grateful, especially Dr. William Fredrickson, Matthew Lata, and Eric Schlossberg.

... an amazing set of people who shepherded this book from its earliest, most disjointed scraps through its final form here—Dr. Mark Rabideau, Dr. Jessica Usherwood, Sylvia Yang, Carolyn Bacon, Peter Sheehy, and Genevieve Aoki—thank you for your patience, guidance, and support through this massive undertaking, and for helping me see this vision all the way through.

... my teacher, David Okerlund, who belongs in every one of the above categories, who has been the most generous and consequential mentor a person could ever hope to have. Coming to Florida State to study with you was one of the best decisions I have ever made, and I owe you a debt I can never repay. Thank you for your friendship, mentorship, wisdom, generosity of spirit, and for seeing something in me when I have struggled to do so. Here's to what's next.

–JH

Introduction

I decided I wanted to be an opera singer in 2011, at the age of 31.

In my early 20s, I was a professional *a cappella* singer primarily in a group called Hyannis Sound, and my experience there inspired me to go to Berklee College of Music and train to be a jazz singer. When I got to Berklee, I realized that what I really wanted to do was use the entrepreneurial and creative energy I already possessed to make sure my talented friends got *paid*. I studied Music Business with foci in Entrepreneurship and Management, and moved to Nashville, where I worked in various capacities in the music industry for over six years—during which time, the familiar twinge came back. To scratch the itch, I sang in choruses, church choirs, and got my first *comprimario* roles at the local company, but I could tell it wasn't going to be enough. It wasn't long before the decision was made for me. One Saturday morning, the day after I was let go from my music industry job, I told Marah, my wife of five months,

> Honey ... I lost my job yesterday—but it's going to be okay.
> I've decided I'm going to be an opera singer.

That she didn't file for divorce on Monday is a testament either to Marah's strong belief in either me or the institution of marriage, but she breathed deeply and told me,

> I don't know what that means for us, but I trust you to figure it out, and to make it work.

Over eight years later, I'm happy to say I vindicated her belief in me, figured some things out, and have managed to work relatively steadily in this industry. Along the way, I learned a lot about the business itself and took much of my formal education out of the realm of theory and into practice. I returned to school to get a master's degree, participated in a couple of Young Artist Programs, and met hundreds of young singers along the way, many of whom had questions about the business that had not been addressed in the course of their education. I started advising those singers and putting together resources to help them. I talked to colleagues in other programs, at other schools, and I realized this was not an isolated situation. I took informal surveys, then a formal one, and interviewed professors and administrative staff at several top voice programs to see what they were doing.

In January 2019, I presented some of my research on professional development and entrepreneurship training in post-secondary voice programs at the National Opera Association's annual conference. Until then, I had been working on this book and the resources on my website entirely based on my personal conviction that many universities and conservatories were not teaching their students what they need to know in order to build their careers in the modern classical music industry. I hoped that presenting my research would give me the chance to plead my case to other teachers of singing; what I found among that passionate and committed group of educators was a full awareness of this gap—and a desire to know how to close it. I spent two and a half straight hours that day talking to people about this research, about what I thought (based on my experience as a singer) singers needed to know in order to navigate their first few years out of school, about how they could access the best possible information for their students. Those conversations gave me a renewed conviction that I needed to finish this book and get these materials together—soon—so they could start making an impact for these teachers and the young singers they are preparing.

At its core, I want to help singers comprehend what they mean when they say "I want to be an opera singer." To that end, I designed this book to answer two broad questions:

What Am I Getting Myself Into?
How Do I Get There?

Part I *(The Industry from 30,000 Feet)* addresses the initial question of "What am I getting myself into?" by describing the structure of the opera and classical music industry and its principal players.

Part II *(How a Young Singer Prepares)* addresses the secondary question posed by Part I: "How do I get there?" If "there" is being an active professional in the industry outlined above, Part II describes in detail the preparation of a singer to enter that industry at the professional level.

Part II also presents another iteration of the primary question of "What am I getting myself into?" by describing the institutions that are in place for developing young singers into professionals.

Part III *(The Nuts and Bolts of Booking Work)* addresses the secondary question of "How do I get there?" in relation to the training programs described in Part II. In this section, you will learn to curate your digital presence and create the professional documents you use to introduce yourself to the classical music world, as well as the process of auditioning for these training programs and professional companies.

Part III also introduces the singer to issues of professionalism in YAPs and main stage work that are most often presumed to be communicated by private teachers or throughout the course of Young Artist Programs—but that I wanted to know before I showed up at my first one. This part is concerned with professional conduct and expectations, as well as ongoing training and what to do if you find you don't want to work or stay within the industry.

I have two goals with this book, and the second one is the one I find most crucial:

1 To teach you, the reader, about the structure of the professional singing world (opera in particular), and equip you with tools and strategies to help you succeed; and
2 To shape your thinking—teach you how to think entrepreneurially and strategically about the business side of your career—so that when the particulars of the business change (and they will), you will know what questions to ask and how to orient yourself so that you can succeed in the next iteration of the business and the one after that.

Each chapter ends with:

1 A Summary of Key Principles to help you internalize the important strategic and developmental goals of the chapter, and
2 Application Questions to personalize the strategy for your own career.

Additionally, most chapters end with:

3 Activities intended to help you build your business based on the discussion in that chapter, and
4 Bookmarks to websites that will remain helpful as you move forward in your career.

If you're having a hard time imagining yourself as an entrepreneur, please allow me to open your eyes: in the United States especially, opera singers must be entrepreneurial by default—save a handful of plan artists at the Metropolitan Opera, and the choruses at the Metropolitan, Lyric and San Francisco Operas, there is no such thing as a fully-employed opera singer. You are always running your own business. You don't have the option to not be entrepreneurial. There. Now let's talk about what that means.

Scholarship on the subject usually defines entrepreneurship as a venture that undertakes significant financial risk while either:

1 identifying an untapped market or need and linking it with a novel idea; or
2 identifying a novel idea and linking it to a yet-undiscovered market.

I think you'll agree that most opera singers do *not* fulfill this definition of entrepreneurship aside from undertaking significant financial risk (both in financial outlay for training, travel, auditions, etc., and in the opportunity cost of forgone salary associated with a steady job). However, in *The Entrepreneurial Muse*, Jeffery Nytch offers an understanding of entrepreneurship as both a *mindset* and a *set of principles*, and the approach that this book offers is aimed at developing in singers both strands of that rope, so to speak.

Why "Operapreneurship," then?

"Operapreneurship" is a made-up word—admittedly a bit of a gimmicky word—that represents a larger truth: like this new generation of singers, it has one foot in the art and another in the business. Singers entering the opera world now have different skill sets, different training, and a vastly different career outlook than their counterparts of only 20 years ago. It is no longer enough to sing and act well; those are the price of admission, the beginning of the conversation. But singers lacking a certain degree of savvy in self-promotion and an understanding of their place in the broader market are at a decided disadvantage in an industry that sees more candidates each year than it could hire in ten. It is expensive to travel to 20 auditions each year, but relatively inexpensive to show a 360-degree view of yourself as artist and person to thousands of people via social media. It is expensive to be a stylistic generalist and present yourself to 10 or 15 companies; it only costs you time and brainpower to research your market—the companies that are most likely to hire a singer with your experience and specific strengths— and select high-probability targets for auditions.

I believe that while not every singer is cut out for creating a new product or a new market, or reimagining the way singers make their income, most can be coached to understand themselves and their place in the broader market (if that's where they want to be) and take steps to increase their chances for success. Not purely a singer, not properly an entrepreneur, but something in between: a singer with an entrepreneurial mindset, who sees the world through the lens of opportunity and who has the tools to orient themselves in the current market and the markets that will follow.

Of course, no book can tell you everything, and there are lots of things that I can't write here by virtue of my still being a working professional in the industry I am describing. But my goal isn't to tell you everything—it's to democratize information that is often siloed, and to prepare you, regardless of where you came from, to approach your career strategically and with the best information currently available. That is the information I have tried to include in this book for you.

This book is, I hope, the start of a conversation that I want to have with all of you. I hope you will stay open-minded, will discuss these ideas with your peers, and that you feel free to contact me and continue the conversation whether you agree or disagree with what I say in the pages that follow this one. In any case, I hope you find something in here that gives you clarity, saves you money or heartache, or just makes you think more deeply about how art and the world interact with each other. This is, in many ways, the best of all possible careers, and if you want it for yourself, I hope you find your way in, and that you'll say hi when you do.

Part I

The Industry from 30,000 Feet

1   Opera Companies

There are, as of this book's writing, over 140 total Opera America (OA) Professional Company Members in the United States across five budget levels. There are at least a dozen more I can name off the top of my head that aren't Opera America professional members, and small companies are cropping up every month, it seems, often with artistic missions that are on the cutting edge of the industry. So it is safe to assume that there are around 200 active opera companies and organizations presenting opera in the United States at a given time, comprising companies with massive budgets and resources (Tier 1—over $15 million/year, including the Metropolitan, Lyric Opera of Chicago, San Francisco) and relatively small budgets (Tier 5—below $250K/year), and everything in between.

Terminology

At some point, you will hear people referring to various opera houses in the following ways:

- "Tier 1/2/3/4/5 House"
- "A/B/C/D House"
- "International/Regional/Vanity Company"

Some of these terms have precise meanings, some have meanings that are a little less precise and more colloquial, and at least one of them is derisive, even if it's descriptive. Let's look at these different groupings.

Tier 1/2/3/4/5 House

As I mentioned above, these tiers refer to Opera America budget levels (see Table 1.1), and the groupings can be seen on their website. These

Table 1.1 Opera America Budget Levels

Tier	Budget	# of OA Professional Companies (2020)
1	>$15 million/year	11
2	$3–15 million/year	26
3	$1–3 million/year	25
4	$250K–1 million/year	53
5	<$250K/year	27

Source: Opera America Membership Directory.

budget levels, available through their annual public financial reports, are as seen above.

A/B/C/D House[1]

These designations used to be rooted in Musical America's budget levels, just as the Opera America tiers above, but now Musical America uses Opera America's classifications in its searchable directory and these designations, persistent as they are, are officially a vestige of another time. Either way, "A" houses are those with the largest budgets (and are presumed to be those with the most prestige) while "D" houses are those with the smallest (and loosely correspond to Opera America's Tiers 4 and 5).

International/Regional/Vanity

These are very loose, unspecific groupings that have to do with who gets hired to sing roles at a given house.

"International" houses regularly hire one or more singers from outside the United States in their productions (which usually means they have the resources available to get visas, pay for travel and per diem, etc.). Here in the U.S., the Met, Lyric Opera of Chicago, Houston Grand, and Santa Fe Opera are examples of international houses. A singer who has an "international" career is someone who regularly sings at this tier of companies and orchestras outside of their home country. (It is *not* a singer who has given a single recital or sung a role in a training program in a foreign country.)

"Regional" houses are companies that primarily hire singers based in the United States, with principal roles typically sung by out-of-town singers who sing full time and *comprimario* roles cast locally. These companies are found at every budget tier, except for Tier 1. If a singer is said to have "a great regional career," it is not derisive: they have probably been singing consistently at some of the best houses in the United States, which is not a small feat.

"Vanity" is a derisive name often used to describe a small opera company whose founder/director regularly casts themselves in productions. I am torn regarding its use—it is no small thing to present opera and trying to do so on a modest budget is difficult. That said, you should still make note of whether a company engages in this practice when you decide whether to audition. Especially if there is an audition fee associated with your application, it's good to know if you're a baritone and the person who runs the company is casting himself as Figaro. But personally, I'd prefer that this term fell out of favor soon.

People/Organizational Chart

At some point, you are going to communicate with someone at an opera company directly, whether through an email or a face-to-face meeting or an audition. When that happens, it will be helpful to know how that person fits into the company's structure. Here are a few of the positions you may encounter:

Artistic Director

The person responsible for the artistic direction of the company. This person has at least some of the casting authority in the company and is likely to be the stage director—or choose the stage director for most or all of the company's productions.

Musical Director

The person responsible for the musical quality of the company. This person is likely to have some casting authority, and probably has significant input into the hiring of other musical staff (coaches, chorusmasters, choristers, orchestra members, etc.). This person is likely to be or hire the conductor for most or all of the company's productions.

Executive Director

Primarily a business manager for the company, setting budgets, fundraising goals, hiring artistic and administrative staff. May also have artistic and casting input, especially in the absence of an artistic director. May also be an important fundraiser for the company.

General Director

Usually pairs the Executive function with one or more of the artistic functions, in place of a standalone Executive or Artistic Director. Like the Executive, the General Director may be an important fundraiser for the company.

Director of Artistic Administration (also Artistic Administrator)

Depending on title and size of organization, may have casting authority, and otherwise performs all administrative functions related to casting, including negotiating and writing contracts, booking artist travel and lodging, and sending direct-casting requests to managers. At most companies, this will be the highest-ranking officer most singers deal with until they are in rehearsals.

Education Director/Studio Manager

The most likely first point of contact for a singer coming out of their formal education. Primary duties typically include casting Young Artist Programs (when YAP serves outreach function); choosing, directing, and booking community engagement programming, including runout shows and public concerts; serving as primary point of contact for Young Artists. A Studio Manager may be used in place of an Education Director at companies without a community engagement component to their YAP, or with a separate Education or Outreach ensemble. (See Chapter 6 for more discussion of YAPs.)

In addition to this top-level staff, if hired by a company, you will interact with some combination of:

- music staff (coaches, chorusmaster);
- production staff (Production Director, Production Stage Manager-PSM, Assistant Stage Managers-ASM, Props Master, choreographer, Fight Director, stagehands, Lighting Designer, etc.); and
- costume/wig/makeup staff (Costume Designer, dressers, Wigmaster, wig assistants, Makeup Designer, makeup assistants);

plus the company's marketing, social media, and possibly development (fundraising) staff.

Though the Metropolitan Opera, Lyric Opera of Chicago, and San Francisco Opera loom large in the American consciousness, the United States is home to some 200 opera companies of all sizes, some of which are pursuing repertoire well outside canonical fare. As you come to understand the variations in size, structure, and artistic mission, it is helpful to gain a sense of which companies focus their energies in your own areas of strength. Most singers in the United States are trained as generalists (i.e. in Mozart, bel canto, Romantic, some Baroque and music of "the long 20th century") but almost everyone has one or more areas of particular strength within their broader aptitudes. If you specialize in certain repertoire, you should spend some time discovering which companies present that repertoire most often and make a note to reach out to the appropriate contact for an audition. In any case, a young singer (like any entrepreneur) benefits greatly from understanding the structure of the business they are entering. But opera companies are just the start of the story; a well-balanced career will see you singing in a variety of venues, some of which we will discuss in the next chapter.

Summary of Key Principles

1 *The American opera ecosystem comprises almost 200 companies.* These companies can be divided by budget level, repertoire, or other characteristics, but above all, the opera industry is not monolithic.
2 *A company's budget level has consequences to what sort of opportunities young singers can find there.* If your local opera company is an international-tier house and you are not an international-tier artist, you many still find an occasional *comprimario* opportunity there, but are unlikely to find stable work there. You are also no more likely to be cast in their YAP because you live in town, though you may be able to perform or cover the outreach tour, if they have one.
3 *Get to know the organizational chart of the opera companies in your area.* It is helpful to know who your most productive points of contact will be as you build a relationship there. For young singers, start with the chorusmaster and Educational Director.

Application Questions

1 Is there an opera company within driving distance of where I live?
2 If so, what budget level is it? What opportunities might exist for me there based on that information? Principal roles? *Comprimario* roles? Chorus? Covers? Outreach?
3 What other companies could I get to for an audition in a three- or-so-hour drive? Answer the same questions as you did for your local company.

4 Who is the person at each of those companies that I should contact in order to audition for the opportunities to which I am best suited?

Bookmarks

- *Opera Careers* (www.operacareers.com)—My website, updated at least monthly, which includes many free resources and pages of links to help improve your research and understanding of the opera industry.
- *Operabase* (www.operabase.com)—The most complete resource in the world for keeping track of the international opera industry. Nearly exhaustive lists of American and international opera houses, managers, and singers, plus season and casting information.
- *Opera America* (www.operaamerica.org)—The best resource for information on the opera industry in the United States. Includes full membership lists in multiple categories.
- *Musical America* (www.musicalamerica.com)—Among the best resources for news about the classical music industry.

Build Your Business

Start Your Opera Company Database. Use Opera America's Membership Directory to make a spreadsheet containing every opera company within three hours' drive of you. Include the names and contact information of the Artistic Administrator, Education Director, and Principal Coach/Chorusmaster. Make a note of what sort of opportunities you're most likely to be hired for there (Chorus, *Comprimario*, Principal, Cover, Outreach/Events, YAP).

Note

1 One of the things I don't like about these designations is that in my mind, A-D are grades one receives in school, and "D" work is bad work. "D" houses are not bad houses—they are houses that make beautiful and vital art with smaller budgets than some other companies. Somehow, I can divorce this logic from Tiers 1–5 above more readily than I can for A-D. Just know that there is exceptional art being made at "D" houses, and it is a privilege to be able to sing at them.

What I am saying here is that to a certain extent, these budget levels seem to correspond (however loosely) to perceived prestige, though there are notable outliers. But it is also important to recognize that "prestige" can be fickle and to the extent that it means anything concrete in the business, it seems to be mostly used by artistic administrators in determining the readiness of an individual singer to take on work at the highest levels in our industry—which comes with higher paychecks and some measure of stability. While it's a useful guide for singers as they develop and move through training programs, obsessing over something as fickle as prestige is a waste of effort, in my opinion. But understanding which companies can provide a sustainable wage or certain working conditions may be worth your while. We'll cover more on that in Chapter 10.

2 Other Performing Arts Organizations

In addition to singing in staged productions with opera companies, you might perform concert or oratorio gigs, be contracted by a festival, participate in the workshop of a new opera, or participate in one of many competitions across the world. This chapter examines several additional types of organizations and ensembles with which a singer might find performing opportunities and suggests strategies for booking engagements with them.

Orchestras

Orchestras provide opportunities to perform some of the great masterpieces of the vocal repertoire: Handel's *Messiah*, Beethoven's *Symphony No. 9*, Mendelssohn's *Elijah*, Bach's Passions, and so on.

One of the great things about these gigs is that they're short—usually just four or five days, including two or three performances—and often provide similar per-service fees to opera without the three-or-more week stay away from home.[1]

Your manager will do their best to book this kind of work for you (and will usually quite deservedly take a higher commission on your fee), but it is scarce, so when you get it,

1 Do it well, so you get hired again; and
2 Get a usable recording (not necessarily to post publicly—as this requires permission from all participants at least, and often is prohibited a union's Collective Bargaining Agreement—but for your agent to pass along to presenting organizations); and—
3 Enjoy it (obviously)!

So how do I get a concert gig if I'm not at the top of the food chain?

I'm glad you asked! There are a couple of steps you can take to increase your chances of booking concert work, whether you're

Other Performing Arts Organizations   17

managed or not. First, make sure you have a good foundation to stand on:

1   Make good, clear recordings of yourself singing concert repertoire (focus on the biggies, and anything that you do especially well, even if it's not as common), including "Pops" repertoire—musical theater, Great American Songbook, patriotic favorites, Christmas/holiday tunes. Whatever you have good arrangements of and perform memorably well.
2   Do great work at all of your opera gigs and research the conductors you work with—if they have a home orchestra, or even if they occasionally work with orchestras, see if there is an opportunity to audition for them privately for concert work. You should do this with opera conductors too, of course, as many regularly conduct orchestras throughout the year.

When you have good recordings and a few standard concert arias prepared:

3   Look for posted auditions for concert work on the big online audition boards (YAP Tracker, Auditions Plus).
4   Reach out to local and regional orchestras in your database—to the Conductor, Assistant Conductor, or Artistic Administrator—with your résumé and recordings (or a URL pointing to them) and ask for an audition, or just for them to keep you in mind. Offer to travel to audition for orchestras within a three-hour-or-so drive from your home base. You never know when a last-minute sub might be needed.
5   Reach out to local and regional universities who have orchestras and choruses that perform masterworks (search the LAO member directory for "Group-University"). Send recordings and résumé and offer to audition. They may not have graduate students or faculty to cover everything they intend to do each year.

As in the opera world, the orchestra world has a trade organization (League of American Orchestras, or LAO) with an online membership directory. At the end of this chapter, you will begin to build your personal database, but know for now that as with Opera America, the League of American Orchestras also divides its members by budget level (into Groups 1–8), and you can search the directory to locate the orchestras in your area by group number, location, or ensemble type.

It is true in this business that *work begets work*, so it behooves an artist to get as many performances of as much different repertoire as possible—even if it pays little to nothing at first, or only covers travel expenses. At the early stages of your career, you are *hoarding* performance experience! Get whatever you can and build your résumé so that you look like (and become!) an accomplished concert performer. That work will communicate to intendants that you are a trustworthy singer who has been hired (and re-hired) by many performing arts presenters for similar work and will beget more work for you.

Festivals

There are many performing arts festivals in the United States that hire singers for more than just opera. Some include opera alongside symphonic works, chamber music, choral works, Pops concerts, musical theater—even straight theater. These can be incredibly gratifying gigs, and opportunities for artistic and professional growth. They can also be harder to find—they often cast directly through agents, existing relationships with singers, or announce auditions on their own website without using one of the bigger audition boards like YAP Tracker.

Concert/Recital Series

Like festivals and orchestras, there are dozens of concert and recital series across the United States presented by different kind of organizations—municipal, commercial, and arts, to name a few. Some of them present recital series in conjunction with a competition (whether live or based on recorded submissions) while others exist for the purpose of presenting exciting artists and innovative programming, including artists and composers from underrepresented populations. The best way I know to find them and their audition information is the aforementioned online audition sites, but you may have some success choosing a city (your home city or one nearby) and doing an online search for "[city] classical voice recital series" or something similar.

Pops Orchestras and Programming

Every Fourth of July the Boston Pops (America's best-known Pops orchestra) performs a nationally televised concert celebrating our Independence Day. The Boston Pops is a bit of an anomaly—very few cities boast their own dedicated Pops orchestra, but many orchestras across the country are adopting programming that prominently features repertoire in the Pops realm: movie soundtracks and scores, Broadway hits sung by stars of the Great White Way, Irish/Celtic/Italian/Latin musics, "Rat Pack" tributes, holiday favorites, and more.

Other Performing Arts Organizations 19

While many programs feature dedicated soloists who tour with a prepackaged show, there are many opportunities for singers who can credibly perform in a multitude of genres. If you want to get in the loop for these opportunities, I recommend taking the following steps:

1 Make recordings (audio, video, or both) of Pops repertoire that suits you particularly well and post them to your website, social media, and YouTube/Vimeo/SoundCloud accounts.
2 Compile a repertoire list broken down by theme, suitable for sending to artistic administrators. Keep it updated with the latest repertoire you've learned and performed.
3 Send audition inquiries to orchestras within a three-to-five-hour drive of your location that perform this repertoire. Include your press kit (Chapter 8), your Pops repertoire list, and links to your videos.
4 Compete in a competition that specializes in this repertoire, like the American Traditions and Lotte Lenya competitions.

In order to sort out which orchestras program this sort of repertoire, just look at orchestra websites and take note of who the singers are on these programs: Are they in your "tier"? Are they singers who tour the entire country singing the same program with multiple orchestras? If not, what is their experience? Did they emerge via YouTube/Instagram? Who manages them? What else do they sing?

Competitions

Competitions, like opera companies, come in many shapes and sizes: some are put on by local or regional presenting organizations or foundations, and some are massive affairs put on by prestigious organizations. Most come with some prize money for the winners, and an application fee for all entrants; some come with the promise of future concerts or paid work, and some are part of a process that leads into a major Young Artist Program. A very few are covered by the press and attended by important industry people like artistic administrators and managers—most are not.

From January 23, 2018 to January 22, 2019, there were 757 listings tagged as competitions on YAP Tracker. Among them were the big ones you may have heard of: the Metropolitan Opera National Council Auditions (colloquially, "the Met Competition"), Operalia, Cardiff Singer of the World, and the George London Foundation competition. There were also hundreds of smaller competitions put on by local Rotary Clubs, city arts organizations, fraternities/sororities, and other arts-interested charitable groups. Making sense of all these options can be difficult, but asking a few pointed questions can help you narrow the field:

1 *What is your purpose for entering a competition?*
 Are you doing it to win some money to help with school? To get feedback on your aria package before audition season? To raise your profile? To what level?
2 *How far are you willing to travel for a competition?*
 Are you at a point where it makes good financial sense to enter a competition thousands of miles from home?
3 *Are all competitions trustworthy or worthwhile?*
 The answer here is a qualified "no," so the singer must be diligent in researching the parent organization of the competitions they consider applying to.

Though many young singers use "opera" as shorthand for their classical voice studies, there is a broad array of performing arts organizations of every size and in nearly every American city where a singer may ply their trade in front of an audience and earn money in the process. While you develop your skills as an opera singer, I encourage you to explore the entire range of musical options available, from Baroque opera to Golden Age musical theater to contemporary art music. It will expand your abilities and artistry and expose you to new career possibilities along the way. Later in this book, we will talk about creating your own opportunities that reflect your unique artistry, but for now, I encourage you to look around at what others are doing in a variety of media and determine whether anything other than opera speaks to you.

Summary of Key Principles

1 *Most "opera" singers don't stick entirely to opera.* Singers who sing primarily in an unamplified setting may sing an opera one month and a concert with orchestra the next. A singer is only limited by their own versatility.
2 *Concert work is great work—it is also relatively scarce.* If you're not on a major management roster, figuring out what you do exceptionally well, making great recordings, and finding opportunities to audition or jump in are the keys to booking these opportunities for yourself.
3 *The market for Pops music is strong and growing—again, versatility is key.* Art song, too, is making a bit of a comeback, and

organizations and ensembles that create interesting programming are finding new audiences and creating greater opportunity for singers.

4   *Competitions aren't for everyone, nor are they a necessary step.* Competitions serve a specific purpose in the larger opera world that isn't necessarily rooted in creating an equal playing field for all singers. Before deciding to compete, be honest with yourself about what you hope to get out of the experience.

Application Questions

1   Besides opera, are there other repertoires that I excel in? Be honest here—this is not a time to list every genre you sing in the car or at karaoke. If it helps, think about how much money you spend to apply and audition for opera opportunities. Do you feel so confident in these additional repertoires that you would willingly spend the same amount to develop, coach, apply, and audition for them?
2   What kinds of (paid) opportunities exist in these various repertoires? Use resources like Musical America to learn about festivals, competitions, and performing arts organizations that might give you a platform for performing these repertoires.
3   How do singers like me do in big competitions? Look at several years of results (if they are available, either on the website or press releases that are still accessible via web) and see if you can identify a pattern.

Bookmarks

- *YAP Tracker* (www.yaptracker.com)
- *Auditions Plus* (www.csmusic.net/tools/alerts/)
- *League of American Orchestras* (www.AmericanOrchestras.org)

Build Your Business

1   *Begin to build your personal orchestra database* using data from the League of American Orchestras' member directory. Focus on orchestras of all levels within a reasonable drive of your home.
2   *Create recordings (audio and video) of orchestral, Pops, or any other repertoire you hope to book* with an orchestra. Make sure they look professional and have excellent sound quality. Show your range and show yourself as an engaging performer; remember that on the concert stage, there are no costumes, no scenery or props, and no special lighting—YOU are the show.

Note

1 Because of that and other factors, many young and emerging singers seem fond of saying, "what I'd really love is to just do oratorio work," when they talk to other singers about their career aspirations. It's a nice thought, but the ratio of days of service to paycheck is the reason almost all of us scramble to find concert work—and why it's so hard to come by. Real talk: most of the mid-sized to large orchestras across the United States hire their concert soloists from the most prestigious management rosters in the business, at least in part due to the absence of a vocal specialist on staff.

3 Management

Part II, How a Young Singer Prepares, introduces managers as part of your inner circle—one of the most important partners in a singer's universe. But what is a manager, exactly? You probably know that they play a crucial role in connecting singers to auditions and work, but what does their work entail? And at what point does their work intersect with yours? Among early-career singers, the topic of management seems to be a source of much interest and precious little information, so this chapter attempts to "flip that script," so to speak, and answer the most common questions young singers ask about management.

Q: What does a manager do?
A: Put simply, a manager works on your behalf to get you (1) access to work and (2) the most favorable contract terms possible. ("Access" is the operative word there—some managers can get you work sight-unseen, but in most cases, you still have to win your work with solid auditions.) But a good manager is also a valuable advisor in your artistic development who knows:

1 the repertoire you should be singing—and are marketable in—now;
2 the repertoire you should be singing at various points in the future;
3 the repertoire that will help you grow from point 1 to point 2; and
4 which companies are presenting that repertoire at strategically beneficial times for the development of your career, and when to put you "in front of" those companies in auditions.

Q: Is that different from an agent?
A: Not in the classical world. Managers and agents serve different—and sometimes legally-defined—roles in the popular music world, but in the classical world, you will hear artists use these terms interchangeably to refer to the same person.

Q: How are managers paid?
A: Managers in the United States are paid in two ways: commissions and retainers.[1] A *commission* is a percentage of the income derived from an artist's work. Most managers charge between 10–15 percent for opera, and 15–20 percent for concert work. A *retainer* is a monthly fee paid to your manager to cover their monthly expenses incurred in the course of working on your behalf. These may range from around $50 per month to $150+ per month, and should include, at bare minimum,

1 an up-to-date page on their website, featuring your bio, audio, video, and photos, as well as your upcoming work and past reviews; and
2 a roughly equal chance at suitable audition and work opportunities that come to the manager.

Regarding the former, it is your responsibility to send them up-to-date media and content for your page. Do this at least twice per year, and more frequently, if your manager asks for it.

Q: When should I start looking for management?
A: Simply put, when you have something to manage. Like any businessperson, managers are wary of high-risk/low-reward scenarios. If your résumé lists only a couple of mid-tier YAPs and one or two *comprimario* roles, you are unlikely to generate attention from a manager, because they are going to have to do a disproportionate amount of legwork to get you auditions and work that generate income for both of you. If you want representation, start building a career that has discernible trajectory, momentum, well-thought-out repertoire choices, and a carefully cultivated image. In other words, do the hard work that indicates that you and the manager are going to have a productive relationship—for both of you!

It may also be that management finds you when you are ready. A handful of major Young Artist Programs and Artist Diploma programs hold showcases, or "house auditions," that are attended by managers and artistic administrators. Your manager may also find you at a major competition or a performance with a professional company, especially in the New York City area.

I'll talk in detail about reaching out to management in Chapter 8.

Q: How do I know which manager is right for me?
A: You probably can't, not with 100 percent certainty, anyway. Finding a manager is not like finding a soul mate—it's finding a business partner. There are likely to be several managers with whom you

would work productively, so I caution you against over-"mysticizing" the process—just do your research and make a logical decision. You should do research to determine things like:

1. Redundancy—Who else on the roster sings your repertoire/projected repertoire (i.e. how many of *you* are there?). Redundancy isn't bad, by the way—you never know how far out the other singers are booked. It's just good to know.
2. Prestige/Room for Growth—Where the majority of the singers on the roster are working. (There is no danger in being the youngest Almaviva on a roster where most of the other Almavivas are singing at "A" and "B" houses; but there may be a real challenge to your career development if they're all fighting to sing it at "C" and "D" houses. There's not a lot of room for you to step into work in your rep when everyone on the roster is on your level.)
3. Finances—Will you have to pay a retainer? What do you get in exchange for it? Can you afford the retainer?
4. Artist Satisfaction—How do other artists feel about the manager? *Do research!* Reach out to singers at or near your level on the roster or talk to them when you work together. Do they feel that the manager is forthcoming and fair? Are there things they wish they had known when they joined the roster?
5. Getting Work—Do audition announcements go out to the whole roster, or does the agency filter internally? Are all artists submitted for auditions who wish to be, or is there a reasonably transparent process for determining which ultimately are? Are there "development" artists (i.e. artists not officially on the roster, but who the manager is "trying out" before signing) in the mix? How frequently do direct-casting or jump-in opportunities come around?
6. Reach—As far as you can ascertain, does the manager have relationships with houses in budget tiers and regions (including Europe, for example) where you want to work?
7. Reputation—As far as you can ascertain, is this manager respected in the industry? Ask trusted professionals and combine that information with what you have gathered about where their artists sing consistently, and you'll have a decent idea of the manager's reputation.

The Artist/Manager Relationship: Artist's Role

Some artists are of the mistaken impression that having management means that they are free to wait around for the phone to ring with a contract offer. Especially early in your career, when your reputation is not doing the heavy lifting for you, nothing could be further from the truth: the manager's value is in the doors they open, the career guidance they give, and the negotiating skills they have. The artist must therefore do everything possible to grow as an artist, to promote themselves, and ideally, to research opportunities that may be off the manager's radar.

It is not enough to say to your manager, "I want to sing three *Messiah*s this Christmas." The better approach in the early phases of your career would be to identify orchestras and choruses within a reasonable driving distance who are performing the *Messiah* (and without named soloists) and to email your manager with those organizations' names, contact information, your recordings, and dates you would be available to audition, if asked. Unless it is a major or regional orchestra, the likelihood of an engagement like this generating substantial commission is low, so if you want your manager to submit a request, do most of the legwork. The request will have more weight coming from your manager, and you will look like a more professional singer in the process.

To this end, it is important that you have great recordings and updated publicity materials (website, résumé, bio, head shots, production photos) so that your manager can send them along to companies at a moment's notice.

The Artist/Manager Relationship: Manager's Role

The manager does have important responsibilities, as well, even if they aren't the ones you might imagine at first. Perhaps the most important responsibility early in your career is offering career guidance: helping you strategize the repertoire that you should be singing this year, next year, in five years … and knowing which companies are performing that repertoire on that timeline. Also, as I mention in Chapter 6, the manager is an excellent resource for knowing the *fach* and specific repertoire in which you are going to be marketable. Many young singers have questionable opinions on the repertoire they should be singing now and later in their careers; the manager can help separate fantasy from reality, and help you start pursuing the repertoire in which you will be competitive at various points in your career.

Additionally, the manager's responsibilities include:

- being present at many auditions and performances for singers on their rosters,
- fielding direct-casting or jump-in requests from various opera houses and orchestras,

- maintaining strong relationships with presenting organizations (this includes sending the best possible artists in response to the aforementioned requests),
- maintaining a website that represents their roster well,
- negotiating contracts,
- communicating artists' on-the-job concerns to presenting organizations,
- cultivating a roster of singing professionals whose work reflects well on the entire roster.

These are the things for which you pay your manager.

Q: *"Can I change management if it's not working out?"*
A: Yes, and you should—but I believe there is a process you should follow, and precautions you should take. As with any business relationship, artist-manager relationships sometimes reach an end to their productivity. And as with any relationship, the participants don't always agree on whether the relationship has reached its logical end. If you are thinking about leaving management, the following is my recommendation for parting ways wisely and amicably.[2]

1. Evaluate the Relationship

When you entered this relationship, you had hope about what it meant for your career. As you became savvier, and grew as an artist and entrepreneur, you re-evaluated how realistic those expectations were, and recalibrated them. Every three to four months, you should evaluate your management situation in this way. Keep your materials up to date, let your manager know if you're working on new repertoire, and check in with your manager to see what they need from you in order to keep you front-of-mind when opportunities come.

As the first year with your manager draws to a close, engage them in a conversation about goals and actionable items for the next year. Always strive to be professional and self-assured, and to assume good faith on your manager's part until you have reason not to. (I don't believe that any manager means to treat an artist unfairly, but it happens, and it should be called out.) Express your desire to work to your mutual benefit, to be a great ambassador for the roster and for yourself and pursue a productive conversation with your manager that leaves you both optimistic for the year ahead.

If at any point you determine that your partnership has reached an impasse, write the reasons down. Set the list aside for a day or two, and come back to it, to make sure that the reasons that are on the list are quantifiable and/or somehow demonstrable through evidence (i.e. they're not just your feelings or suspicions—these aren't invalid, but are hard to back up if a conversation should become contentious). Then, bring that list to your manager.

2. Address Your Concerns to Your Manager

When you have determined the reasons you feel it is time to move on, set up a one-to-one conversation with your manager, via phone, video conference, or in person. The tone of this conversation should be neither accusatory nor defensive, but reasoned and constructive. *You have a business you're trying to run, and you recognize that they do, too, and that they have other artists to look after, but you have a few concerns that need to be addressed.* If you are willing to remain in the relationship, and particularly if you are paying a monthly retainer and have evidence that you aren't being treated fairly, you should also make a list of actionable items that your manager can complete to demonstrate their desire to remain in your employ. This is the time to present those. These might include:

- updating your page on their website,
- plugging your important upcoming work on social media,
- attending your performance in their area (especially if you feel it will show them something they don't already know about you as an artist),
- listing opportunities or companies to cold call for you.

Put a time frame on these items and stick to it. Be reasonable ("a house audition at the Met within three months" is not necessarily a reasonable demand), be prepared for every possible response, and most of all, be prepared to walk away if you determine that you are truly at an impasse. It may be that your manager has soured on you, and it may well be your fault in some way. Whether or not it is, the productivity of the partnership is most certainly expired. Get out, for both of your sakes.

3. Determine Your Remaining Responsibilities to the Partnership, and Get Them in Writing

You are under contract. Perhaps it is a one-year or multi-year commitment, and perhaps it is an at-will, month-to-month contract. Regardless of the particulars, you likely have responsibilities to your manager at the end of your time together—commissions on future work that they negotiated or obtained for you, or perhaps some sort of "buy-out" of your remaining retainers. (You might owe a penalty for breaking your contract, which will amount to some multiple of your retainer, up to the remainder of the contract's duration.) Ideally, there will be no penalty for terminating a partnership that is unproductive for both parties; just read your contract and be prepared for any possibility. Do not make threats, and do not tolerate their being made against you.

A Word of Advice on Pursuing New Management

If you are under contract with management, you are not forbidden in any way from pursuing a more suitable management situation. Read that again. While some managers may be squeamish about appearing to "poach" clients, most will hear you and speak with you about the possibility of joining their roster and consider your existing representation a benchmark of professionalism. If you want to pursue new management while under an existing contract:

- Be discreet. This is probably not the time to put out public feelers. This is a very small world.
- Be candid with managers about your current situation.
- Be honest, if understated, about your reasons for wanting to leave. Remember that if you throw your current manager under the bus, this manager will assume that you will do it to them, too. Present yourself professionally, with forward-looking reasons for moving on. *Do not engage in gossip.*
- If they want to sign you, be thorough and forthcoming about your responsibilities to your existing management, including the engagements for which they are owed commission.

Final Thoughts on Management

As it is with the teacher, the partnership with management is a crucial one for singers; a good manager can bring tremendous value to an artist, and vice versa. As with a poor teacher, a lesser manager can contribute to your wasting several good, productive years pursuing repertoire for which you are ill-suited, or contributing in no perceptible way to the growth of your career. Similarly, because they deal with essential questions of your artistic viability as separate from your self-worth or individual artistry, your manager *must* be someone whose judgment you trust and respect, and from whom you can take hard criticism. The day may come when they have to tell you something you are not prepared to hear, and a good manager can help take the sting out of some unpleasant truths, so work very hard to build this relationship into one of mutual respect and mutual benefit. As I stated in the beginning, you alone are ultimately responsible for determining what is best for your career, and for entering into and terminating partnerships according to the benefit they bring you. You should do this wisely, soberly, and after thorough research and analysis.

Summary of Key Principles

1 *A manager is a* partner, *not a* patron. A manager amplifies what is already working. There is no sense looking for management when you don't have career momentum, and as an early-career singer, your own hustle doesn't end when you get representation. Continue to build momentum that they can amplify.
2 *Having no management is better than having bad management.* If you are unrepresented, the worst that can happen is you don't grow, don't get exposure, don't get guidance. If you are poorly managed, your manager can burn bridges you never knew about, or otherwise reflect badly on you as an artist and professional. Do your research.
3 *Constantly evaluate your management situation to see how it can be better.* If there is something you can be doing that will help your manager serve you, do it. If there is something they can reasonably be doing to help you, tell them. If the partnership becomes unproductive or contentious, there is no shame in either of you ending it; if you can do so amicably, all the better.

Application Questions

1 Am I ready for management? Does my career show both promise and momentum that would attract a manager? Do my other advisors believe I am ready?
2 What should I expect of my manager, and how involved do I need to be once I am on their roster?
3 If I am being asked to pay a retainer, what do I receive for my retainer? How do I know if I am receiving anything? Is my retainer an advance that my manager must recoup (less common), or is it in addition to the commission I pay (more common)? Is there ever a time with this manager that I will be exempt from this retainer?
4 Does my manager take a percentage of everything I do, whether they are involved or not? Is there a lower threshold below which my manager won't take a commission? If a request for work

comes to me through other means, and I pass it along to my manager to negotiate, and the bottom line doesn't increase, does my manager still take a commission?

Bookmarks

- "Roster Change" page at Musical America (www.MusicalAmerica.com/pages/?pagename=latest-roster-changes)

Build Your Business

1 Do some research on managers: find out who manages your favorite singers, your friends, and other singers you have worked with. Look at their rosters—are you a fit for this roster at this stage of your career?
2 Read Kristina Driskill's excellent interview with Alex Fletcher (Fletcher Artist Management) at www.gildedwithin.com/audition-secrets-fletcher-artist-management
3 Find one or more listings of managers who represent singers in the United States. Options include Operabase, OperaCareers.com, Musical America. Look through their rosters to see who they manage and where those singers work.
4 Use your research to make a mental list of three to four agents you may be reasonably ready to approach in a year or two.

Notes

1 I covered the topic of retainers in some depth in an article on my website: www.operacareers.com/retainers
2 N.B. Nothing stated here constitutes legal advice. If you believe there has been a breach of contract on the part of any party in your situation, you should seek legal counsel from an attorney who specializes in contracts.

Part II
How a Young Singer Prepares

4 Formal Training

The 21st-century singer who aspires to full-time engagement on the operatic stage has no shortage of obstacles to that goal: financial pressure, shrinking budgets at opera companies that imperil both training programs and length of seasons, and companies that increasingly skip New York audition season and hire off familiar management rosters or through hometown auditions, to name a few. Despite all that uncertainty, there is a measure of consistency in the pursuit of an operatic solo career, and that is the roadmap itself.

True, many singers come to their careers outside of this map, but you will find that prevailing wisdom suggests the vast majority come to their full-time careers in roughly the manner outlined in Figure 4.1.

Clear as mud?

The first four stops on the path shown here concern a singer's "formal" training—that is, the externally organized, rather than self-directed aspects of preparation that a singer undertakes under the close guidance and mentorship of trusted professionals. *Most* professional singers you encounter will have gone through at least three of these four, and, anecdotally and perhaps intuitively, it seems that either Pay-to-Sings or graduate school are the most likely to be skipped.[1]

Wide is the Road; Narrow is the Gate

But while the road map in Figure 4.1 is technically correct, I think its complexity obscures a higher order that is more helpful to understand. The milestones listed here can be grouped into two broad categories: *Formal Training* and *Professional Work*.

As you can see in Figure 4.2, this common progression moves through three distinct phases:

- the singer pays for the opportunity to learn and perform;
- the singer is paid to perform while receiving advanced training; and
- the singer is paid to perform as a professional main stage artist.

36 How a Young Singer Prepares

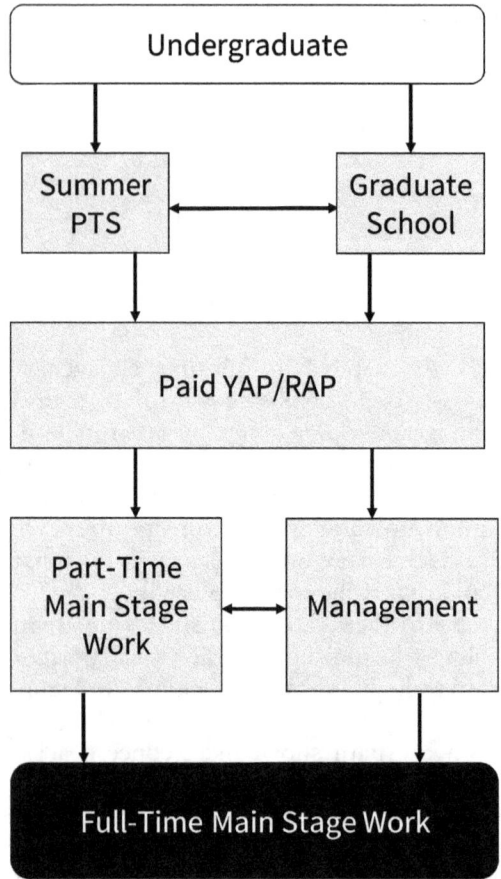

Figure 4.1 The Opera Career Roadmap

Notice that YAPs and RAPs are a pivot point of sorts between formal training and professional work. (This will be covered at length in Chapter 5.) This illustration helps to communicate an essential truth about building an opera career in the 21st century in the United States: that YAPs and RAPs are the real proving ground—the true gatekeeper, in other words—for most operatic careers. Everything that comes before them becomes less important to your career because of the access, training, exposure, and performance opportunities YAPs and RAPs provide. If a singer approaches this cynically, they can tell themselves that access, starting with educational institutions, is more important to career success than skill or talent. I think this is true to

Formal Training   37

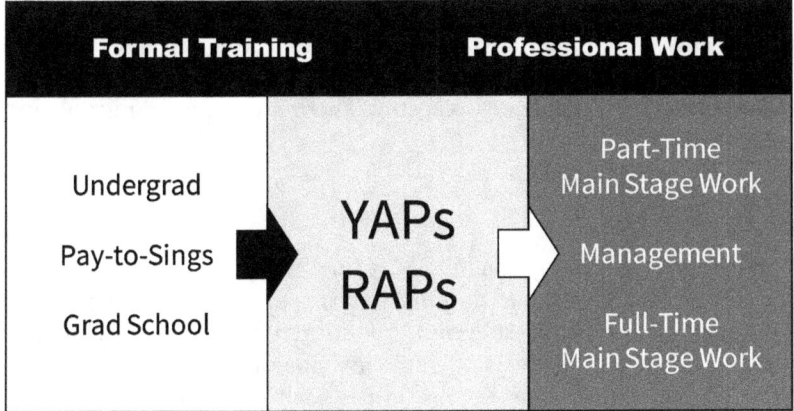

Figure 4.2 The Opera Career Breakdown

an extent, but prefer to see it[2] as a challenge that may be unlocked by thorough research (Chapter 7) and entrepreneurial strategy, provided the requisite levels of skill and artistry are in place.

Formal Training Venues

Undergraduate Degree

There are successful singers with every manner of bachelor's degrees: mathematics, foreign languages, English, criminal justice, physics, political science, music education, instrumental performance—and, of course, vocal performance. When you're young, the key is finding a voice teacher who can build your voice in a healthy, sustainable way. If you can also get some stage experience, whether in opera chorus, musical theater, *comprimario* roles in an opera, or community engagement productions, all the better. I also highly recommend, if nothing else, taking some languages and diction courses if your school offers them. Some graduate schools require a year of language and a semester of lyric diction in each of the three major singing languages (Italian, German, and French), so if you can make a dent in those requirements in your undergraduate work, you should. It will save you time and money later.

Summer Tuition-Based Training Programs (*"Pay-to-Sings"*)

These will have their own section in the YAP chapter (Chapter 5), but these programs are a very common first foray into the world outside of academia as a singer. Offerings vary, but you will find a mix of language, acting, and movement training alongside lessons, coachings, master classes, and perhaps business seminars. You may also perform in concerts, scenes programs, or possibly your first full main stage roles, either with piano or orchestra. There are many in Europe and many more in the U.S.

Graduate School

Not everyone goes to graduate school, nor should they—but graduate school can be a very beneficial time in terms of growth as a singer, not only from a technical standpoint, but from an artistic one. It is here that many singers get to sing their first major roles, roles that will form the core of their repertoire in the early stages of their careers. Additionally, and anecdotally, what I learned in my vocal pedagogy class and through teaching singers in my assistantship helped me internalize the things I was learning in my lessons, and I think it really accelerated my progress. Your mileage may vary.

But with any higher education comes the matter of finances, and especially debt. If you took out a lot of loans for your undergraduate degree, graduate school may only be a possibility for you if it is fully funded (tuition/fees/health insurance) with an assistantship (which typically carries a small stipend or salary in exchange for teaching or administrative duties). Be honest with yourself up front about your financial bottom line, and what you can afford to invest in a graduate program in terms of financial outlay (tuition/fees/living expenses) and opportunity cost (the income and other financial benefits you forgo while you go to school). If you don't find the right program or get the right offer, there's always another year. Do not fall into the trap of incurring unaffordable debt because you fear the offer in front of you is the last one you'll ever receive. Take another year of lessons and preparation and if you still want to go to graduate school. You will be a stronger candidate for it.

Paid YAPs/RAPs

These programs are the ones you've most likely heard of, and they will receive a thorough treatment in Chapter 5, but these are paid programs attached to professional opera companies where young singers often draw their first real wages as singers, get their first "covering" (that is, understudy) experience, and have their first main stage experience alongside world-class singers.

They are also, as I mentioned above, often a place to make an impression on important administrators, coaches, and conductors who may open doors later in your career.

Undergraduate Teachers

It is my strong belief that the primary function of the voice teacher at the undergraduate level is to guide the student in building the healthiest technique possible and pursuing the most beneficial performance and learning opportunities to prepare them for the next step. If you are a high school student looking at programs and teachers for your undergraduate degree, reach out to teachers and find out what their teaching philosophy is, where their former students have gone to graduate school, which summer programs they typically recommend their students attend. If possible, also take a trial lesson with teachers you are seriously considering. It is important to know how and whether their teaching style fits with your learning style.

Focusing on these questions, rather than the most extreme career achievements, helps you understand how well the instructor is preparing students at your level. The rest can wait for graduate school inquiries.

Graduate School Programs and Teachers

Graduate school presents a whole new level of questions and considerations, all of which should be thoroughly answered in the course of deciding where to apply. Among them:

1 *What do you want out of your career?*
    Do you want to be a full-time opera singer? Do you want to be a voice teacher? Do you want to teach in college, high school, or in private practice? Each of these suggests potential exit points from the academic credential ladder.
2 *Which credential should you pursue, based on your career aspirations?*
    Options include M.M. in Voice/Opera, Artist or Performer's Diploma (AD/PD), D.M./D.M.A., and Ph.D. In all but the rarest cases, the AD or PD is designed to follow the M.M., so it may not be available unless you first undertake the M.M. One notable exception is the AD at Academy of Vocal Arts (AVA) in

Philadelphia. This is a four-year diploma credential that prepares singers for performing careers.[3]
If your goal does not include teaching at the university level, your formal training will stop at the M.M. or AD/PD level. If you wish to be competitive for teaching at the university level, Master's to doctorate is the most direct path.

3   *What do you need from a voice teacher?*
The conventional wisdom is that you choose a graduate school for the teacher above all other considerations. I agree with this for the most part; the teacher is the most consequential figure in the early success of the singer, and so this relationship should be the primary consideration in choosing a graduate program.

4   *What gaps are you hoping that graduate school will fill?*
If you need performance opportunities above all else, it may not help to look at small programs without main stage opportunities. Then again, if you have a popular voice type, a smaller program with voice-type balance may give you more opportunity than a larger one. If you want to be able to do singing work outside of school without traveling, look to big city schools where you could potentially get educational or community engagement work with a local company, or solo/paid chorus opportunities with small local orchestras or opera companies. If you need to use graduate school to sequester yourself and focus exclusively on technique, you may benefit from being in a smaller city or college town in order to remove the temptation to do too much outside singing.

5   *Is the timing right?*
Are you choosing graduate school because you're in a rut or need a change of pace? To rekindle or reconsider your interest in singing or singing-adjacent things? If you're looking at a M.M. or AD in the hopes that it will jump-start your career, ask trusted advisors about your viability and what you can reasonably expect to gain. Unlike our instrumentalist colleagues, different voice types and different singers take different periods of time to mature; while a well-prepared soubrette soprano or a Rossini tenor may be ready to enter the YAP/professional circuit at 24, a contralto or bass may not be "settled" until well into their 30s.

6   *What can you afford?*
The reality of higher education in America is that some students are priced out of some opportunities. That goes especially for singers, very few of whom will make an income that permits

them to repay significant student loans, and so singers have to be especially sensitive to and clear on what the financial requirements of their chosen program are.

As you build a list of potential programs, you should reach out to the music admissions office and/or the voice area to learn how and to what extent graduate students are funded. The answer will rarely be a one-size-fits-all package, but here are the factors to ask about:

- Tuition Remission: Full tuition? Partial tuition? At some state schools, graduate assistants (not all grad students) are coded as in-state students for tuition purposes. This matters if you go over your allotted credit load.
- Fee Remission: Even if your tuition is fully covered, many schools have per-credit and other fees that the student must pay. These fees can be over $1,000 per semester. How are they covered, if at all? Does the student pay out of pocket? Does the department provide scholarship funds to cover them?[4]
- Health Insurance: How much of the school's health insurance requirement will you be required to pay out of pocket, versus how much is included in your assistantship?
- Scholarships: What is the average scholarship amount, above and beyond the assistantship?[5] Are there requirements tied to that money? (e.g. Are you required to audition for main stage productions and/or required to accept whatever role is offered? Are you then restricted in which YAP/Professional auditions you can be released for?)

Choosing a graduate program is a multi-faceted research project that you should take very seriously. I recommend beginning the process of exploration no later than the early spring of the year you intend to apply. Applications are almost all due on December 1, so this timeline allows about four to five months of research (including calling school offices and sorting out application and prescreening requirements) and two to three months of gathering documents, recordings, and recommendations. It also allows you time to save up the money you'll need to apply and audition at your chosen schools (a process that can easily cost $750 or more per school, when you factor in application and transcript fees, airfare, hotel, pianist, and food).

The decision to undertake formal training is a personal one, and while it is not a requirement in order to have a singing career, the vast majority of American singers who ultimately rise to the level of a full-time domestic or international career do complete at least one degree or diploma in singing and participate in one paid Young Artist Program, so dismissing this phase wholesale is a risky decision, given the odds. But do your best to take advantage of opportunities to gain complementary skills or knowledge bases. Acting, yoga, dance, movement, and even martial arts are pretty obvious candidates, but imagine what you could bring to Shakespearean characters with expertise in British theater or literature; or to any of opera's great military figures with advanced knowledge of history; or to productions of your own creation with expertise in design; or to your teaching studio with intimate knowledge of vocal anatomy and function. There are so many possibilities to make yourself more well-rounded and more compelling as an artist, entrepreneur, teacher, impresario, or whatever shape your career takes. My advice is to use your time in higher education and beyond to learn things that make you come alive and help you be a more complete artist, one who stands out from your peers at every stage.

Summary of Key Principles

1   *Higher education for singing is not for everyone*, but it is helpful to most. Between the time it affords a singer to focus on technique, learn and perform new roles, and explore other areas of interest, it has the potential to pay off significantly *under the right financial situation*.
2   *YAPs and RAPs are the most common and important proving ground for the 21st-century opera singer*. Of all of the opera world's various access points, YAPs seem to provide the most complete opportunity to advance to the next level.
3   *A singer's voice teacher is the most consequential figure in their career*. Finding one who can help you build a technique that sustains you is worth more than 100 master classes or one-off coachings could ever be. This consideration should supersede all others when choosing a graduate program, especially.

Application Questions

1   In what area(s) of artistic development am I lacking? Can I address this/these effectively through private, à la carte study, or am I better served by pursuing a more comprehensive training program?
2   If I am best served by a comprehensive program, what type of program should I explore? Should I pursue one that gives me

short-term training in a few key areas (e.g. a summer Pay-to-Sing), or one that gives me a broader, deeper exposure along with performance experience and long-term coaching (e.g. a Master's degree or Artist/Performance Diploma)?

3 If I choose higher education, what does my current financial situation say about the kinds of programs I should pursue?

Build Your Business

1 Start building a database of YAPs, Pay-to-Sings, and graduate programs (see Chapter 7) you think may be good fits for you. Include information about financial packages and other factors that are important to you, like performance opportunities. Gather all of your unanswered questions about each program and call or email the program administrator to get clarification.
2 Start a list of things you want to learn in order to become a more complete artist and person. Keep this note somewhere easily accessible—such as the Notes app on your phone, or an app like Evernote—so you can reference it and take note of opportunities to fill in those blanks.

Notes

1 There are also a couple of common shortcuts for a VERY few singers. These include prominent competitions and post-undergrad training programs (like AVA and a couple of notable Artist and Performer's Diplomas), and when I say they're a rare workaround, I mean *very* rare. As such, I'll mention them in the context of a singer's training, but I won't spend much time on them, as that can be a bit like saying, "to be debt-free, just win the lottery, then pay off your creditors"—not technically incorrect, but not really a plan you can put in front of a mortgage lender.
2 And here I speak as a cis-het bass, just to acknowledge my own privilege.
3 Artist and Performance Diplomas are not academic credentials, as such, so they do not meet most schools' requirements for Doctoral admissions, should you wish to pursue that path. Nor are they technically a "terminal degree," which may be important should you later apply for an academic job. This is the topic of an ongoing discussion in professional voice teacher forums, and I agree with the perspective that they are best understood (as with the M.M. in this discipline) as "trade" degrees—that is to say, they are geared toward applied work in the field of singing, rather than the academic study of it.
4 If the latter, be sure that you don't work these funds into your budget as income.

5 Some institutions may keep these numbers close to the vest, but it can't hurt to ask. And if the Admissions or departmental offices themselves don't want to share the numbers, you can ask around or perhaps even get this information from a faculty member (it will be less precise in these instances, but a ballpark figure can still help you get a workable idea).

5 Non-Academic Training Programs
PTSs, YAPs, and RAPs

It is exceedingly rare, though not entirely unheard of, for a singer to progress directly from their academic training into a main stage career in opera. For the majority of singers, the years during and immediately after your academic training will be characterized by participation in non-academic programs of various sorts. In this chapter, you will learn about the various kinds of training programs and the most common singers you will find in them. You will also begin to answer important questions for yourself, including:

1 Is the opportunity in front of me worthwhile?
2 What area of my artistry needs the most attention, and where can I best address that?
3 What experience or opportunity should I pursue now in order to reach the "next level?"

Non-Academic Training

Admittedly, many people would prefer to be done with formal training after their academic degrees are finished, but the physical and artistic demands of singing opera, plus the reality of a competitive job market, exacerbated by the huge number of university voice programs compared with the relatively small number of opera companies necessitate an additional "proving ground" of sorts. In the medical world, that proving ground is called a residency. In the opera world, it takes the form of non-academic training programs in a few varieties.

"Pay-to-Sings": Tuition-Based Training Programs

The first iteration of these programs that most singers encounter is the tuition-based programs we refer to as "Pay-to-Sings." Broadly speaking, these programs tend to be in the United States or Europe, last between two and eight weeks, feature faculties from American universities, and usually provide:

- lessons (one or two per week)
- coachings (one or two per week)
- language/diction classes
- classes in scene study, movement, yoga, Alexander Technique, and/or stage combat
- concert opportunities
- scene work
- fully staged opera performances (often double- or triple-cast, with piano)
- audition master classes
- an introduction to the opera business.

Here, a singer often gets their first look at what a career in singing looks like: living out of a suitcase, meeting new people, seeing new places, rigid rehearsal schedules with big blocks of free time, trying to budget while you go without income for an entire production period (we'll talk about this in Chapter 10, when we build your business), and the bittersweet experience of leaving a new group of people to return home or join your next cast.

These programs are early résumé-builders: they cater largely to singers who either have not yet completed their academic training or have recently finished it (within one or two years) and/or have very little solo stage experience on their résumés, and often provide some of a singer's first experience performing complete roles on stage. A young singer may also have their first experience "jumping in" as a cover for an unprepared or indisposed colleague, so if you are cast as a cover in one of these programs, let this be your first reminder: be ready when your number is called.

The price tag can be steep, though: some programs run more than $5,000 before scholarships are calculated, and don't include whatever travel arrangements a singer incurs in getting to the program's location—but the best ones can easily provide that much value to a young singer. The trick is to know which ones are reputable. To learn that, ask around: Facebook singer forums have several threads devoted to good and bad experiences at specific programs, and are full of singers who have attended before you. If you're curious, ask![1]

Programs to Watch[2]

If you're making a list of programs to look at closely, there are several long-standing and highly regarded programs that not only provide

Non-Academic Training Programs 47

training and performance opportunities, but can really deliver on giving you connections and a platform as you try to launch into the YAP arena. Among these (not an exhaustive list): Seagle Music Colony, Aspen Music Festival, Janiec Opera Company at Brevard Music Center, Opera in the Ozarks, OperaWorks, and CoOPERAtive. Among the newer crop that provides a high level of training in multiple areas are: Hawaii Performing Arts Festival,[3] Miami Summer Music Festival, Spotlight on Opera, Pittsburgh Festival Opera, and Russian Opera Workshop.

The list of European programs is very long, and of similarly variant quality. My advice here is again to ask around on Internet forums to see who has a reputation for truly delivering on their promises, and who may be more interested in funding a vacation for themselves and their friends on the backs of young singers and their families. Programs run by an American university (e.g. the Frost School's program in Salzburg) and famous programs like AIMS Graz are very safe bets with reputations established over decades.

Specialized and Non-Opera Training Programs for Singers

In addition to the wide variety of opera-focused training programs, there are programs for art song (e.g. SongFest, Ravinia Steans Music Institute, Fall Island Vocal Arts Seminar), language immersion (Middlebury Language Schools), dramatic voices (Institute for Young Dramatic Voices), chamber music (Marlboro Music Festival), and other specialties.

Tuition-Free Tuition-Based Programs

There is a very small subset of these tuition-based programs that bears mention here, and those are the ones that don't pay, but are also essentially tuition-free. These programs have top-tier staff, high production values, and are as close as you can get to being in a YAP without being in one. They include:

- Music Academy of the West (Santa Barbara, CA)
- Tanglewood Festival (Lenox, MA)
- Ravinia Steans Music Institute (Highland Park, IL)
- Fall Island Vocal Arts Seminar (Potsdam, NY).

YAPs (Young Artist Programs)

Young Artist Programs, or YAPs, have become a bit of a catch-all term for any singing-related program a "young artist" might go—but that is a misnomer. The term Young Artist Program is best understood as referring to a program that:

- pays you to sing,
- is attached to a real, functioning, paying opera company,
- provides training,
- includes performance assignments like outreach, covers, chorus, small *comprimario* roles, scenes, and concerts,
- once again, *pays* you.

The first American Young Artist Program was founded at the Santa Fe Opera by John Crosby in 1956 to nurture the next generation of great American opera singers. His innovation became the model for not only American YAPs, but the *Opernstudio* programs in German-speaking theatres as well, and the Santa Fe Opera Apprentice Singer program remains one of the standard-bearers for artist training in the United States to this day.

The YAP experience is a crucial part of the development of most singers in the United States; it is in these programs that most young singers first hear a world-class voice, and get to watch how a world-class actress sings, moves, and comports herself among colleagues and company leadership.[4] At its best, it is a formative experience that teaches singers professionalism and gives them real responsibility for representing themselves and a company in public performance and social events. At its worst, it is cheap labor for a company that helps it achieve its artistic goals, whether it delivers training or not.[5] As with most things, the majority of experiences likely lie somewhere equidistant between decently paid artistic nirvana and soul-crushing sweatshop labor.

RAPs (Resident Artist Programs)

Another distinction that is worth making considering more recent industry trends is between Young Artists Programs (which focus primarily on training and outreach) and Resident Artist Programs.[6]

Resident Artist Programs, or RAPs, are a subset of YAPs, the distinction being in how the artists are utilized by the company. A Resident Artist Program, as such, uses its artists as a sort of house "ensemble"—akin to a German *Fest* ensemble. There is little to no focus on training; the ensemble is there to perform principal roles on the main stage in exchange for regular wages.

There is a predictable effect to this philosophy, and that is that these programs *tend* to cast older, more experienced singers, rather than those just out of school, because they need to be ready to perform in the company's productions from the starting gun.

Tiered YAPs

One final program type is something of a hybrid of the YAP and RAP: a tiered program where the lower tier trains younger singers, gives them small covers, and utilizes them in choruses and outreach; and the higher tier casts more experienced singers in main stage productions and gives them top-level cover duties. If you can get into the lower tier as a younger singer and make a good impression, it will likely give you an inside track to being cast in the higher tier when you are ready.

Examples of tiered programs may be seen in Table 5.1.

The YAP World is Not Fair

I think this goes without saying, but the YAP world is not fair. I had a conversation with an amazing friend and colleague recently that elucidated this point for me, especially as it pertains to sopranos. And since statistically speaking, more sopranos are reading this book than any other voice type, I feel the need to say this: while the YAP world is not predictable for anyone, statistically, it is especially difficult for the YAP system to treat sopranos fairly. YAPs provide experience through three main vehicles: chorus work, *comprimario* work, and cover work. Because of the way most canonical repertoire is set up, there are hardly any *comprimario* roles (early-career résumé-builders for most, and meaningful career tracks for some) written for sopranos, and that has consequences for your résumés, among other things.[7] This means that even when you beat the massive odds to get a YAP position over hundreds of your peers, you are likely to be limited in the main stage opportunities you can undertake.

Table 5.1 Tiered YAPs

Company	Lower Tier	Higher Tier
Chautauqua Opera	Studio	Apprentice
Sarasota Opera	Apprentice	Studio
Wolf Trap Opera	Studio	Filene Center
Teatro Nuovo	Apprentice	Resident Artist
Palm Beach Opera	Apprentice	Young Artist

I don't know how to fix this so long as most opera companies commit most of their resources to producing canonical repertoire—but I thought in the interest of being honest, it was important to note.

A Word on "Connections"

Every industry has its gatekeepers, and opera is no different. It is also true that opera has its fair share of people who would exploit a young singer's naïveté for their own personal gain. In order to best protect yourself from exploitation (in any way, including for your artistic or emotional labor), you need to know that:

- With all due respect to the many wonderful faculty members at these programs, the number of people working for tuition-based programs whose influence in the industry can substantially impact your career for the good or the bad may be counted on roughly two hands.
- The Metropolitan Opera is a massive organization, and very few people who have ever worked there seem to be able to pull any meaningful strings on your behalf. Those who can, have likely held long-term positions on Artistic Administration staff.
- Most of the people you work with at these programs mean well—but what they see from you is a tiny slice of what your teacher and coach at home know. *Do not* make massive changes in technique or repertoire based exclusively on dramatic pronouncements made in coachings or master classes. There are no shortcuts. Test everything against what you know works for you.

All of this said, the best advice I can offer you is that you draw very firm boundaries around yourself—know whether you're willing to let someone play around with your hard-won technique just because they hear or want to try something. They're not around for the fallout when your technique needs rebuilding. Be open to trying things but put up boundaries and respectfully but firmly defend them if they are pushed against. We all want to be told we're special, that there's a place in the opera world for us, that someone appreciates what we're doing—but at what cost? As a professional singer, you will have to establish boundaries—around your technique, your beliefs, your marriage and/or family, your financial situation. Start establishing them now, and you will be building a muscle that holds incalculable value for your career.

#metoo Goes to the Opera

(Trigger Warning: sexual assault, rape)

Any discussion of boundaries and exploitation in opera or elsewhere now exists in the context of a broader movement that has at last given voice to the innumerable singers who have been victimized in myriad ways in the course of their work. As the #metoo movement—a 2006 social media campaign supporting women of color who were sexually abused—gained a wider constituency in 2017, many powerful men in Hollywood, politics, academia, and yes, opera, were outed as and accused of being serial abusers. Opera's turn happened quickly and decisively, as some of the "worst-kept secrets" in the business began to find a voice, and the perpetrators of alleged abuse were brought into the light. One of the world's most famous conductors and several prominent singers and directors were among those named, and many of their alleged victims are still waiting to see if they face consequences.

As in so many of the cases brought to light by the #metoo movement, these involve a significant power imbalance that is all too common in the operatic world: an established, popular, and powerful man and a woman or man (often an artist whose career is not yet established) whose livelihood and bodily autonomy are threatened through no fault of their own by the impossible scenario thrust upon them. I say "all too common" because of the precarious nature of opera's Young Artists: they live on the razor's edge financially, attend dozens of auditions from which they are lucky to book one or two paying gigs, are constantly made aware of the younger and "hungrier" singers coming up behind them, and they face an industry that uses them as "young" (read: cheap) artists well past any reasonable definition of the word. So when they finally get their break, the heartache and trauma that may accompany not just the assault itself but the ensuing self-interrogation ("Was I really good enough to get this gig or did they just like the way I looked?") is unimaginable and unconscionable.

But these violations don't always assume a form as obvious as some of the stories in the media. A casual survey of dozens of singers revealed a laundry list of disturbing behaviors (all inappropriate; all reportable) that our colleagues have endured throughout their careers:

- kissing/touching beyond agreed-upon limits on stage (when a reaction would interrupt the scene);
- physically interacting with singers (principal or chorus), especially in staging intimate scenes, without permission;
- commenting inappropriately on a singer's appearance, personal life, etc. (Abusers use your reactions to such comments to ascertain your boundaries, that is, what they can get away with. Make sure they know the answer is "nothing.");

- telling a singer they can't say "no" to direction given on stage, even if it makes them uncomfortable. (This often implies one can't say "no" offstage, either, without retribution.) This is known as "grooming" behavior, and its intent is to condition you to accept further abuse.

If you wish to work in this business, *do not* engage in any of these behaviors. If you observe these behaviors, you should report them.[8] Note: In many public cases of this nature, the alleged aggressors and/or their supporters have made something of a sport of asking the accuser to consider the effect such (true, by the way) allegations might have on a distinguished career. Do not take this bait. Your abuser gave no similar thought to the effect of their actions on you. Your humanity and your hard work entitle you to an equal pursuit of a distinguished career of your own, and you are not required to sacrifice autonomy or psychological well-being to earn it.

Resources for Underrepresented Singers

The opera world—especially in the United States—has not always willingly made space for singers from underrepresented groups. It is discouraging that in 2019 we have conversations *around* and pertaining to underrepresented singers without an accompanying effort industry-wide to bring more of our excellent colleagues into the fold. Several times each year, it seems, singers of color are asked to weigh in on a controversial production of *Porgy and Bess*, *Aïda*, or *Otello*—rather than just being cast in them. Singers of Japanese, Chinese, Korean, and Vietnamese heritage (to name a few) are indiscriminately interrogated about their feelings on an ill-conceived production of *The Mikado*, *Turandot*, or *Madama Butterfly*. These microaggressions pile up in the psyches of our colleagues as we fumble through these debates with and around them, all the while failing to make space for their talents to be rewarded on stages across the country.

That said, there are a few notable organizations that work to promote underrepresented singers in opera and classical music generally. Among them:

- Sphinx Organization
- Young Arts
- The McCleave Project at Opera Memphis
- Marian Anderson Award through the Kimmel Center (Philadelphia)
- National Association of Negro Musicians (NANM) and Vocal Competition

Non-Academic Training Programs   53

- The Legacy Project through National Opera Association
- Classical Singers of Color Resource & Support Group (CSCRSG) on Facebook
- 3arts (Chicago)
- Harlem Opera Theater (NYC)
- Houston Ebony Music Society
- Videmus.

Note: Not all of these organizations work exclusively for the benefit of underrepresented singers, but all are committed to the promotion and advancement of underrepresented groups.

Charting Your Course

Though "YAP" has to some extent become a catch-all term, it is important to differentiate among the different kinds of training programs—in order to target your applications to the correct category of opportunities, yes, but also to see how the industry has structured itself over time to prepare singers in a deliberate progression from their student phase to their professional career. Whether you are an undergraduate student looking at your first tuition-based training program or a second-year graduate student wondering if this is the year you will finally apply to Merola or the Ryan Center, you stand the best chance when you have ascertained what each program does for and expects of singers and match that thoughtfully to your experience and preparation.

In Chapter 7 you will learn how to thoroughly research and orient yourself among your options, but for now it is enough to understand what sorts of programs exist in the broader context of the opera industry and what function they serve. Stay attuned to the programs that feature less or no opera performance component—these are designed to fill in blanks in your training or heighten your level of artistry in some area, whether language, movement, textual study, or song literature. There are more programs than any one singer could ever experience, and each person's progression is slightly different. Take time to evaluate your options and consider what you stand to learn in various places and lay out a strategic approach to becoming the best possible singer you can.

Summary of Key Principles

1 *Singers' non-academic training comes in two broad categories: the kind you pay for, and the kind for which you get paid. The bar*

for entry is set accordingly, and has to do with a multitude of factors, not the least of which is readiness for professional main stage assignments.
2   *When you are paying for training, make sure you get what you pay for.* Many young singers don't feel entitled to make demands, but short of making demands, consistently reminding a program of the promises it made can help ensure you get your money's worth.
3   *There are dozens of YAPs at different levels with different responsibilities, and they are an important stepping-stone.* Do your research (see Chapter 7) to determine whether you meet the program's requirements before applying to save yourself time, money, and frustration. Every program is not for every singer.
4   *As a general rule, don't believe anyone who tells you they can get you jobs.* Those who can, typically don't have to tell you about it—and why would they, unless they were trying to exert inappropriate influence? Ask around if someone makes these claims to you. Sunshine is the best disinfectant, and simply asking someone else in administration or music staff could potentially derail this behavior.
5   *No one has a right to touch you, comment on your appearance, or condition hiring or favorable work environments on receiving sexual or even social attention from you.* Most companies now have sexual harassment policies in place and policies for reporting violations. Unfortunately, some companies still choose to side with the alleged aggressor and terminate the singer. Colleagues, if you want to be an ally, you may consider offering to report the offending behavior and risking being fired yourself. It is extreme, yes, but white men in particular enjoy a good bit of privilege in this business and we should be willing to risk it in order to bring about the structural change necessary for our less privileged colleagues to flourish.

Application Questions

1   If I am being asked to pay thousands of dollars, am I getting thousands of dollars in value? Setting aside the allure of being in Italy or Germany for a summer, what am I getting for my money, and are those things that I value most in writing?
2   Is a full role in a Pay-to-Sing better for me at this point than a chorus-and-cover contract with a smaller paid YAP? Why or why not? (Hint: Look at gaps in your experience/training.)
3   How might I discern I am ready to sing for Merola/Santa Fe/HGO/Lindemann/Ryan Center?

4   Which YAPs are willing to take a singer with no professional experience?
5   What are my personal boundaries pertaining to my voice, my career, my psychological well-being, and my bodily autonomy? How can I prepare myself to confront or manage those who try to encroach upon them?

Bookmarks

- American Guild of Musical Artists Sexual Harassment Policy & Information Portal (www.musicalartists.org/faq-help/help-page/sexual-harassment-policy-information-portal/)—This page contains not only the portal for reporting violations but AGMA's (the American Guild of Musical Artists) official sexual harassment policy and several articles about abuse of various kinds.
- The American Paid YAP List (www.OperaCareers.com/YAPListOriginal)—An original resource I created in 2017. By the time of this book's publication, it will contain a wealth of data on over 60 American Young Artist Programs, including salary and benefits, work assignments, housing and travel information, and much more.
- TrueLinked (TrueLinked.com)—A European job board that specializes in "jump-in" casting, but also does a good bit of principal casting at houses of all sizes across Europe. Really only useful if you are already working in Europe. Owns and is integrated with Operabase.

Build Your Business

1   Go to the websites of several programs of each type mentioned in this chapter (if you need inspiration, look on YAP Tracker or Auditions Plus) and read their "About" statements to get a sense of what kind of singer they cater to, then look at their old audition and season listings to see what sort of repertoire they favor and what kind of singer they accept. Use this information to make a list of possible application targets this season, next season, and two seasons out.

Notes

1   Search the forums first. Many of your questions will have been asked multiple times in recent months, and different groups of people contribute different knowledge to each thread.

2 These are not endorsements, per se, but acknowledgements of reputations over time. There are other programs I could have named, of course.
3 The author has previously served on faculty at Hawaii Performing Arts Festival.
4 I am hesitant to implicate myself in this way, but I do want to share a moment that to me illustrates the magic of encountering world class singers in this setting. In my first summer as an apprentice at Santa Fe Opera, I was singing a small role and covering another in a beautiful Tim Albery production of Strauss' *Capriccio*. The cast was full of brilliant people who were also brilliant singers and watching them converse among themselves and with Albery as they prepared a scene and worked through the dense, intricate text was something I will never forget. At one point, though, I fixated on this mezzo-soprano who was so keen, so quick-witted, so fully committed to her character, I caught myself thinking, "Who *is* this amazing artist? The world *has* to know about her!" The world did; it was I who was in the dark. The mezzo was Susan Graham, one of the greatest in the known universe. And I can only say, in light of my embarrassing naïveté, that in her case and so many others, the hype only barely does her justice.
5 I am not thinking of any companies here, just mentioning what a bad experience might look like.
6 It is worth mentioning that these distinctions aren't always followed precisely by companies: some call their RAPs YAPs, some call their YAPs RAPs, and some call their YAPs and RAPs Studio programs. The point is, when I use these terms, I also try to provide a meaningful definition that distinguishes among duties and experiences a singer might have in one of these programs. It is more important that you, the singer, understand these distinctions than that the industry adopts this nomenclature.
7 My first summer in the Santa Fe Apprentice Singer Program, I had *seven* assignments: two small roles, two medium-large covers, and three choruses. That was one of the busier contracts, but it was not unique. By contrast, while there were sopranos and mezzos who had some cover and main stage duties, several soprano contracts that summer were two choruses, total. It wasn't for lack of trying, of course—the administration at Santa Fe works hard to ensure that the apprentices get meaningful experience. It's just math.
8 At the time of this book's publication, reporting channels for sexual harassment and abuse are decentralized and not as clear as we in the singing community would like. AGMA, our labor union, has established a reporting portal for members who would like to document an offense, and this is a good step, but it leaves many singers without a similar clearinghouse. We are working on it, we promise. In the meantime, most companies you work for will include reporting protocols in your orientation materials or cover them at the beginning of your time on-site. Please do not be afraid to utilize them—they are there for all of our protection, and it will be harder for the offenders to hide as time goes on and more light is shed on their actions.

6 Your Team

In the course of your formal training, you begin to develop your personal artistry as well as a sense of your personal "brand" (i.e. who you are and what you offer to a world full of singers). You also begin to build your team: your most trusted group of advisors whom you will lean on for advice throughout your career.

Matthew Epstein, who has served as an artistic advisor to companies including Santa Fe Opera and Lyric Opera of Chicago for some 40 years, in addition to running Welsh National Opera and the Vocal division at Columbia Artists Management (formerly CAMI), calls this your "Board of Directors"; my teacher calls it your "inner circle." Whatever you choose to call it, these people are essential players in the life of a professional singer, and they serve distinct and complementary roles in your professional life as long as they are around. They are people who can open doors, who can offer you the benefit of their experience as professionals in the field, and who can guide your repertoire choices, and they are the people who will celebrate your professional and personal success with you most profoundly—because they have watched your development, seen your work behind the scenes, and they know better than anyone what each success means.

Building Your Board

So who are these "directors" who will help you navigate your future in the opera business?

1   Your teacher
2   Your coach
3   Your manager
4   Your significant other.

As in any business, choosing your inner circle is an important—even sacred—thing. Take the process seriously and pursue it strategically and organically. Look for team members who have experience to offer you, with whom you work well, and who are committed to your success.

Your Teacher

Perhaps the most important professional relationship in a singer's life, your teacher is the steward of your vocal development and health, the person who knows the technical aspects of your voice better than anyone, and a guide who can either bring your voice to its full potential or leave you stagnant and frustrated. The teacher is, in many cases, the source of most of the information you receive on the business of being a singer, and an important conduit for learning the history of the business and its major players, as well as which roles in the repertory are good fits for your voice at various stages.

You may find that different teachers suit your needs at different stages of development. This is okay: you are the one who is ultimately responsible for choosing. You should stay with a teacher as long as the relationship remains productive, or until life circumstances make continued study with them untenable.

Your Coach[1]

Your coach is responsible for preparing you in dramatic intent and context, style, matters of language, and diction. They are usually gifted pianists (sometimes conductors, too). Some great ones possess an encyclopedic knowledge of the repertory and can suggest new roles or audition arias that are well-suited to your voice. They may also be your most important collaborator, appearing with you in concert, recital, and important auditions in cities all over the world. A great coach is invaluable to a singer, so if you find one, invest in that relationship, learn all you can, and work toward your greatest possible artistic collaboration.

Your Manager

Your manager comes a little later in the game, often after you have already made some good and bad choices, sung some roles professionally, and have your voice built to a point where you consistently produce at a high level of quality. While the teacher helps you know what repertoire you are capable of singing, and a coach can help you find repertoire that suits you musically and dramatically, your manager brings to the table a very important perspective: the repertoire in which you are marketable, that you can get *hired* to sing.[2] Further, the best ones have a broad knowledge of the development of various singers' careers, can help you plan your repertoire development over several years, and importantly, knows which companies will be presenting that repertoire at key points in your development.

Because of this knowledge, the relationship with your manager has the potential to be the catalyst for your "breaking out," or can be a constant source of frustration and disappointment for you, if your manager lacks both the knowledge and the influence that make them valuable. Choose this person wisely—whose careers have they built? Have they helped build the career of a singer like you? Where are their singers singing? What is their reputation?

This relationship is a *partnership* that many singers mistakenly believe to be one-sided (i.e. the manager works on behalf of the singer, and auditions and contracts show up as a result). The reality is that, especially at the entry level, your relationship with your manager is one of partner-partner, not patron-benefactor, and requires at least an equal amount of work on the singer's part in order to be successful.

Your Significant Other

You may be surprised to see your significant other on this list of artistic and career advisors, or perhaps you already understand the way their input informs the development of your career. It is important to acknowledge the extent to which every decision you make in your career affects your significant other—financial considerations, time apart, future implications of current work, to name a few notable ways—and to seek their input. But they can also be an important partner in another sense: if they have reliable ears, they may be able to provide feedback to you on a more regular basis (especially when you're traveling for a gig) than your teacher or coach.

If you trust your partner's ears, and they are up for the challenge, consider having them sit in on your lessons as you prepare a role with your teacher. They will learn to hear your voice the way your teacher does, to hear what fatigue, over-darkening, pushing, carrying too much weight, and other issues sound like in your voice, and can let you know (even in real time—via text, for example) at a performance if one of these performance-killers is creeping in.

Others

Most singers will be well served by this group of advisors and will never have need of another layer. That said, maybe there is an important mentor in your life who is not necessarily in the opera world but always helps you clarify your thinking in important matters; maybe you're fortunate enough to have a handful of coaches or conductors who know you well and are invested in your success; or perhaps you decide to hire a publicist or marketing expert to help with your self-promotion. Whoever this next layer contains, just be wary of "input fatigue."[3] This is why you should always be clear in your mind as to who the "inner circle" comprises and what function the group is meant to serve.

I have some strong feelings about these roles that I'll share below—with the understanding that these are just my opinion, and you should let them guide your thinking only to the extent that you share my values in this area. Above all, as with any relationship, these require trust and good faith from both parties. My advice to you is to avoid hasty decisions if you feel like replacing one or more of these people—as in any relationship, tremendous growth can come from disagreement. Be honest and seek to understand. The process of learning is messy and frustrating, but so is the process of making art.

Additional Thoughts on Your Inner Circle

- Either your teacher or your coach should have spent time around working professional voices, preferably at larger houses. How else will you know whether you are making a sound that is suitable for the relatively large theaters—even at regional houses—in the U.S.?
- Your manager should have solid knowledge of singers, houses, and repertoire. Ideally, they can tell you from experience what repertoire you should sing in the coming years, what you will be marketable in, given progress in certain aspects of your artistry. They should know the difference between the singers required for, for example, the Rossini Bartolo and King Filippo II. They are both basses, but they are not sung by the same person.
- Your teacher should also have a sense of where your voice will "go" and a plan for getting you there. You should see progress over time (months, not weeks), and have a candid relationship with them that allows for honest assessment of your progress. It is likely time to move on if the relationship becomes competitive, contentious, or abusive in any way.
- I would be wary of any teacher who, early in our relationship, tried to redefine me in terms of *fach* or repertoire without giving me a detailed explanation of the factors that contribute to their conclusion. Many well-meaning teachers have reassigned a *fach* for a student who merely needed a different technical approach to the

repertoire they were already singing. For more information on *fach*, check Richard Boldrey's *Guide to Operatic Roles and Arias* and the Kloiber *Handbuch der Oper*, which is the definitive guide to the *fach* classification system and its usage in German-speaking countries.

As a singer progresses in their career, they will encounter many people who will offer guidance and feedback in order, ostensibly, to help the singer progress. But too much input, and from people who don't know your voice, your artistry, and your person well enough, can throw a singer off course before they realize what has happened. The antidote to this situation is to cultivate an "inner circle" of people who know you and your voice best, and who have your best interests at heart. You should work deliberately to have this inner circle in place as you begin your career, and evaluate its members honestly as you go; there will come a time when the circle may grow to include multiple people in the same role, or that one or more people may need to "cycle out" and make way for someone else whose guidance is more immediately relevant to you. Stay open with your inner circle and honest with yourself and make sure that this circle of trusted advisors serves your needs as you progress in your career.

Summary of Key Principles

1 *Singers should have a trusted "inner circle" of advisors around them* to help them navigate important career decisions.
2 *The essential members include your teacher, coach, manager, and significant other*, but other layers may include trusted mentors outside of opera, duplicates of the core group, or professionals who serve other professional purposes (e.g. marketing, promotion, branding).
3 *The specific people in your inner circle may change as you evolve in your career.* That's okay—strategy and organic processes contribute to this change, just as they do in all areas of our lives.
4 *At least one member of your inner circle should have an active connection to the opera industry* so that you have accurate information to inform your deliberations.

Application Questions

1 Who are the people who currently constitute my "inner circle?"
2 What are their strengths/weaknesses in terms of this group's function (this could be inaccessibility/busyness, a lack of access to current information, etc.)?

3   Do I have at least one person in my circle with top-level opera experience (either performing or working with singers) to help guide my repertoire choices? If not, what would it take to add someone like this?
4   Who might I seek out in order to add them to my inner circle, or to build a working relationship with to ensure that I have the best available information around me as I make career-related choices? (Think about teachers/coaches connected to local or important opera companies, for example.)

Notes

1 It is worth noting that in the parlance of popular, amplified genres, people who call themselves "vocal coaches" usually function the way our voice teacher does. That is not the coach we're talking about here.
2 Anecdotally, I think *fach* is one of the most misunderstood and abused concepts in the singing world, and unfortunately, I believe it often begins in the studios of well-meaning teachers. But the *fach* system in Germany was created as an administrative tool, not an artistic one; it made it possible to distribute the roles in a season in a balanced manner among the company's professional (*Fest*) ensemble, not to guide singers toward their ideal repertoire. (To wit, Nick Shadow in Stravinsky's *The Rake's Progress* is listed as a dramatic baritone rather than a bass, even though his highest note is an E4 and the tessitura of the role sits quite low for a baritone. But the ensemble bass sings Father Trulove, so the baritone gets Shadow.)

In my mind, it is best to think of *fach* as *descriptive*—i.e., what you have sung, especially repeatedly—rather than *prescriptive*—i.e. what you should sing. You should sing what you can sing comfortably, and let companies hire (and rehire) you based on what they hear, not what you tell them. In any case, I beg you to disregard all advice found online that seeks to advise you through or toward a *fach* change based on any criteria but those that have to do with your technical suitability for singing a given role.
3 See Chapter 5.

7 Research

The previous chapters have been devoted to teaching you how the industry is structured (Chapters 1, 2, and 3) and what some of the traditional access points are (Chapters 4, 5, and 6). Your next step is to begin to understand that whatever your virtues as artist, entrepreneur, and human may be, they are ultimately attributes of *You: The Service*.

Angelica Richie wrote a piece at the end of 2019[1] that challenged the prevailing artist-as-entrepreneur language that pushes artists to think of themselves as products. Her point boils down to this: products *do* while services *are*. Put another way, products are *disposable*, while services are *adaptable*. Doesn't the latter sound more like an artist? We learn, we grow, we adapt, we create value. We aren't simply different flavors or colors of the same interchangeable good, nor should we encourage the sterile commoditization of our artistry by marketing ourselves as such.

As a service provider, you must approach your market strategically: you wouldn't tell an ad buyer to "put this ad on the Internet" and expect much in return. Marketers use complex analytics to place their ads where they will have the greatest impact. Singers can also manage their financial and emotional resources by casting a smaller net in a strategic area where they have the highest chance of success.

The tool for closing this gap in the case of both the marketer and the singer is research: gathering, organizing, and analyzing data dispassionately. If you learn the right questions to ask at this point, and where to find and analyze information, you will have developed a skill that will help you build your career long after you've graduated from the YAP circuit.

What Kind of Information Do I Need?

I love data. My entire life is in spreadsheets—or everything that can be meaningfully captured in one is, so it will come as no surprise that

I recommend a series of spreadsheets as the primary organizational tool for a singer's career. I use Google Sheets for all my career-related data because it can handle the fairly low-grade calculations and formatting these subjects demand and they can be easily shared with friends and colleagues should you decide to combine or disseminate your efforts. So what sort of databases should you keep?[2]

Company/Contact Database[3]

Probably my most important database is the one I use to track all my auditions. At this point, I have four years of data on every person I've sung for to help me gauge my chances of booking work in different places and when it is time to reach out for another audition.

The sheet is set up with the following column headings (in order):

1 Contact Name
2 Company[4]
3 Email
4 Audition 1 Date
5 Audition 1 Location
6 Audition 1 Feedback/Result
7 Audition 1 Follow-up
8 Audition 2 Date
9 ... etc.

The setup is as simple as it is crucial, and the format is meant to reflect something else that is very important to your ongoing professional growth: the understanding that it is *people* and not *companies* that hear you. It is people, not companies, that hear and remember your auditions and track your growth. So the first column is the *person* and you should change the company name to reflect where they currently work—and many of them will change at some point during your career.[5]

You may also decide to keep only one column for feedback, either containing all feedback in chronological order or just the most recent (and relevant).

Graduate School/Artist Diploma/Fellowship Database

If you are considering going back to school, whether to work on technique, to pursue a credential toward future academic employment, or any other reason, the list of criteria for choosing schools to apply to and attend can be long and somewhat convoluted. Here is the format I used recently when I applied for graduate programs:

Tab 1—Program Data

1. Personal Rank
2. School Name
3. City
4. State
5. Degree
6. Program *(e.g. Opera / Performance / Pedagogy / Performance & Literature)*
7. Teacher(s)
8. Tuition Waiver *(Full + Fees / Full—No Fees / Less-Than-Full)*
9. Stipend
10. Duties Tied to Funding
11. # of Funding Years *(look for two for MM, three for DMA)*
12. # of Full-Time Coursework Years *(important if you're interrupting a performing career)*
13. Total Credits
14. # of Recitals
15. # of Main Stage Productions per Year
16. Dissertation/Research Document Required?
17. Policy on leaving for work *(important if you want to take external work while on assistantship/fellowship).*

Tab 2—Application Materials

1. School Name
2. Application
   a. Applications Open Date
   b. Music School App? *(Y/N)*
   c. Due Date
   d. Separate University App? *(Y/N)*
   e. Due Date
3. Application Fees
   a. Music School
   b. University
   c. Prescreen *(very rare)*
   d. Audition *(very rare)*
4. Supporting Materials
   a. References *(#)*
   b. Pre-Screen Recordings *(Description: 3AS/2A = three Art Song, two Aria)*

    c   Personal Statement *(Y/N)*
    d   Transcripts *(Official/Unofficial—most require unofficial for the application)*
    e   Other *(e.g. may include résumé, repertoire list, writing samples, a specific essay).*

Tab 3—Prescreen/Audition Repertoire

It may be helpful to put these on the same tab, one on top of the other, because the columns will typically be identical.

1   School
2   Art Song
    a   German
    b   French
    c   English
    d   Italian
    e   Any *(covers language like "four total, including one each of French and German"—in which case I mark one each under French and German and two under "Any")*
3   Arias
    a   20th/21st Century
    b   18th Century *(or "Baroque," or any other period specified)*
    c   Recitative *(rare)*
    d   Oratorio
    e   Any *(same as in Art Song)*
4   Notes.

Tab 0—Application Process (Optional)

If you also want to track your application processes in your spreadsheet, you may want to look at using a Gantt chart template, as I did, which allows you to track progress visually. If you want to use a less flashy approach, you can build a similar tool in Excel; the idea is to track every deadline in the process and track interdependencies of various tasks (i.e. sending prescreening recordings is dependent upon both choosing and recording repertoire according to requirements, and each task should have a deadline that reflects that, plus a margin for error). You really don't want to neglect to tell your recommenders that one of your schools has a due date two weeks earlier than the rest.

PTS/YAP Database

This database should probably be new every year (or at least a new tab in the same sheet). The format is similar to the graduate school sheet.

I recommend you visit my YAP Database and just scrape the most recent data, then delete the programs that don't apply this year. You may also choose to use a weighting scheme like the one I describe in the endnote related to graduate school program data (Tab 1).

Review/Press Database

In order to keep your website and professional materials up to date you will need to keep a current list of your reviews on hand. You may find it's better to just keep a Google Doc or Word document with these reviews rather than a spreadsheet. Here's what to keep track of:

1   Production/Dates
2   Company/City
3   Reviewer/Publication
4   URL/Date Accessed
5   Complete text of passage including your name or reference to you.

See Chapter 8 for information on excerpting reviews.

European Audition Database

If you decide to go to Europe to audition, you should create a database of current contacts both at opera houses and management firms. I have these in one database on two separate tabs. Both sets of data may be obtained from Operabase, but the *most* up-to-date information is behind a (very modest) paywall on the German site for the *Deutsche Bühnen-Jahrbuch* (DBJ, or German Theater Yearbook).

Know Thyself

Gathering data can be grueling, but it's basically simple. The next step is the hard part: Self-Assessment.

One of the first things we need to wrap our heads around as we prepare to take our service to market is our level of preparedness—and this can be very difficult to discern, especially in isolation, so there may be some trial and error early on. The reason for this is self-evident: our goal is to position ourselves strategically so that we save ourselves effort, money, and some degree of psychological distress in the course of applying for opportunities to move forward as professional singers. Some bigger-picture questions are easy to answer: most singers aren't ready to be heard by the top programs right out of their undergraduate studies, and many aren't ready immediately after graduate school, either. It's a progression by design. It can be helpful, then, to plan to start at a lower rung in order to get experience and feedback about your next step. Prior to that external feedback, though, knowing how your experience stacks up to singers in the programs you're looking at can give you important context.

Document Your Experience

This step requires taking an objective look at your résumé (if you don't have one yet, we will create it in the next chapter) and gauging the significance of each line. It may be helpful to "code" each line based on certain meaningful criteria, for example:

- Solo/Ensemble
- Lead/Supporting[6]
- Opera/Operetta/Musical Theater/Recital/Choral/Other
- Orchestra/Chamber/Other
- Performed/Coached/Learned.

If this seems impersonal, it should. When we are building ourselves up as artists, we need to love and nurture ourselves; when we are gauging the market for our services, it helps to be as dispassionate as possible.[7] We can't count on every casting director being as enamored of us as we are.

Collect Feedback

Find every opportunity to receive feedback from people with relevant expertise—this may include:

- your teacher
- your coach
- other coaches you work with
- conductors (at university, Pay-to-Sings, apprenticeships)
- any casting director who is willing to give feedback (this is not particularly common if you are unmanaged)
- professional artists you work with (ask to sing for them!).

This feedback is crucial to orienting yourself in the industry, in terms of repertoire and opportunities; it makes it possible to make strategic decisions even if you don't come from a major program in a major city with constant access to professionals.

Beware of "Input Fatigue"

Young singers are especially prone to what I call "input fatigue" (also: "paralysis by analysis" or "too many cooks")—where a person receives so much feedback from so many people in so many settings, without prioritizing or sorting that information according to relevance, that they become paralyzed by the sheer volume of conflicting advice and opinions. This is precisely the reason a young singer needs a trusted team around them: to sort through feedback according to content and source and determine whether it is useful to the singer's development. Remember that many people who give you feedback have known you for a much shorter time than your team, and usually only in one specific context. It is your team that can help you sort through the good, the bad, and the superfluous so that you can integrate only the most helpful feedback as you grow.

Now that you have examined your own experience, it is time to apply the same principles to opportunities you want to apply for.

What to Look For[8]

Let's do some research on YAPs for this year's round of auditions. Admittedly, this can feel a little strange, but continue to reassure yourself: you are an entrepreneur conducting market research for a product into which you have invested tens or hundreds of thousands of dollars and countless hours. Knowing the market is essential.

After you have a list of programs to target, go to the websites of those YAPs and see if they list their singers. If they do, see if they include a biography or list of previous experience. If not, do an Internet search ("singer name + voice part", "singer name + opera", "singer name + school", etc.) to see if you can find that information through those means. If this search doesn't yield something, move on to the next singer—research on 40–50 percent of the singers should start to paint a picture of the type of singer who generally gets accepted to this program. You need not write all of this down—just read several biographies or résumés and get a general sense, then make a note of whether your experience compares well to the participants in each.

There is no set rubric here: a singer's experience is one of several factors that YAPs (and companies generally) use in screening applicants. What we're looking for is a ballpark sense of equivalency in experience.[9] So if it seems as though most singers in a given program have more experience than you, try moving down a budget level (or to Pay-to-Sings, if you were looking at Tier 3/4/5 houses). If you're more experienced than most, see who is engaged by the YAPs at the next level up. If you're right in the middle, make a note: companies on both sides of the divide are probably good candidates for an application.

Leave No Stone Unturned

Once you have done some research on the singers in various YAPs, it's time to turn to perhaps the most consequential people in the process: the program directors.

As I learned in the course of auditioning for dozens of programs, many of the directors of the most influential YAPs have given detailed interviews over the years, some of which cover artistic and technical philosophies in their selection processes. This information was meant for public consumption, so not reviewing these interviews in the course of your research would be, in my opinion, inexplicably negligent. Why would you not want to know, for example, that the director of a program you are targeting is skeptical of candidates who offer Verdi or Wagner before age 30? Or how someone examines a singer's breathing and other technical aspects of singing in determining their suitability for the program? So learn the names of the top-level staff at each program and spend some time searching for instances where they discussed selection criteria or their concepts of good singing—and use that information to further narrow your list and optimize your audition strategy.

Application Requirements: Screening at the Company Level

Often, companies try to help their potential applicants self-select in or out by including a profile or set of experience requirements in their application listing. If the program requires a graduate degree (rare, but it happens), don't bother applying until at least the second year of your Master's. If it says something like "Must have spent at least one year in a YAP," you're likely to get screened out unless you've done at least a partial-year YAP or a prestigious summer YAP, but may still get screened out if you don't have a full year in aggregate. (There may also be exceptions if you are otherwise known to the company.)

There are reasons for these requirements, and they are usually very practical: as I mentioned in Chapter 5, many companies now treat their YAPs as Resident Artist programs, using their Young Artists in main stage roles, and casting slightly older singers than the average YAP. In this case, the company must know that you have experience on stage and can be trusted with that sort of assignment. If you are not at that level (and again, be honest), it is probably wise to look at other YAPs where your responsibilities will include outreach, concerts, covers, and *comprimario* roles, and plan to apply to these bigger YAPs when you have a body of work to attest to your abilities.

Ancillary Benefits of Research

This discipline of research in your field will pay dividends in ways you probably haven't considered. For example, if you're just coming out of undergraduate studies at a relatively small school (even at big ones!), you may not know what options exist for your next steps—that teachers matter, that schools matter (less so, but they undeniably open doors). But maybe you notice that four of the Young Artists at Central City or in the Gerdine program went to the same graduate school, and maybe even studied with the same teacher. Maybe you notice that school/teacher combination pop up in a few more programs, and so now you determine that you should go take a trial lesson with that teacher and apply to that school. Maybe further down the line, you notice that three of your favorite singers, or two of your favorite colleagues from a production you did are on the same management roster, and so you resolve to reach out to that manager for a consultation or audition in a year or two. These are all scenarios in which thorough, ordered research can be leveraged to your advantage.

So, research, research, research! Equip yourself with as much knowledge as possible, and allow your questions to lead to further questions, and then: build a strategic plan with the information you find.

Summary of Key Principles

1 *A strategic singer understands the market that they are entering.* This includes institutions, access points, and people of importance, but also the values and pain points (needs) that guide their decision making. When you understand their needs, you can better position yourself to meet that need.
2 *Keep your audition and research data organized* in a system that serves you. If not my system, start from the kinds of data you need to organize and build a system that does what you need it to.
3 *Take time to honestly assess your experience and preparation* and use that information to strategically plan your application season.
4 *Don't assume your initial assessment (of anything or anyone) is correct.* Ask questions, and then ask the questions that naturally follow those questions. Keep asking until you run out of answers, then ask someone else to fill in the blanks or correct your thinking. Be so inquisitive it annoys you.

Clarifying Questions

1. What kind of programs am I hoping to apply for in the next two to three years? Graduate school? Pay-to-Sings? Paid YAPs? What are the most important program-specific factors to my development? How can I best determine which programs in each category will be most beneficial and appropriate based on those considerations? (This tells you what kind of data to seek out and prioritize.)
2. Who else in my voice type is doing these sorts of programs? What can I learn from their experience that will help me better assess my readiness for or interest in these programs?

Bookmarks

- AGMA Schedule C (www.MusicalArtists.org/contracts-and-agreements/schedule-c/)—Breaks down canonical operas into role classifications based on workload: Lead, Featured, Secondary, Bit, Chorus Bit. Used in AGMA contracts for setting minimum pay scale for each role; useful to non-union singers in negotiating their own contracts.
- Airtable (www.airtable.com)—A powerful, free database website that facilitates powerful inquiries across multiple spreadsheets (essentially "pivot tables") which are useful for tracking information with multiple interdependent categories of data (i.e. a very good place to build your Company/Contact Database). Import/export-friendly.
- *Deutsche Bühnen-Jahrbuch* (www.Buehnengenossenschaft.de/bjbbo/scripts/clsAIShopBO.php?cmd=Search)—The German Theater Yearbook. A directory of staff members at German-speaking theaters. Useful for making contact with theaters and requesting auditions.
- Future Met Wiki (www.FutureMet.fandom.com/wiki/Future_Met_Wiki)—Crowdsourced site that tracks rumors regarding future season programming at the Metropolitan Opera. Interesting to singers who want to audition at the Met for particular seasons.
- Musical America "People Moves" Page (www.MusicalAmerica.com/pages/?pagename=peoplemoves)—The best place to track the moves of administrators at classical music organizations.

Build Your Business

1. *Build out the databases that will serve you immediately* and populate them with the most complete, current information you can find.

2 *Research five or six YAPs you are considering auditioning for*—see if they list their Young Artists on their website. Do a cursory search of a few names to see if you can get a sense of the experience that most participants have before being accepted, and how your experience compares.

3 *Examine your résumé* and begin assessing the quality of the experiences you have had through the eyes of someone hiring for various opportunities. Can you find opportunities to fill in a gap or two this year in time for audition season?

Notes

1 Read it here: https://medium.com/@angelicarichie/the-product-fallacy-7de4f5f9f87f

2 Examples of each of these may be accessed at my website, OperaCareers.com

3 In Chapter 1, you created a "Company Database," and naturally, this one sounds like a duplication of effort. As your career goes on, this "Company/Contact Database" will be the primary thing to which you refer and the "Company Database," if you choose to keep both, will come into focus as one of strategic targets for auditions/communication. To that end, it makes sense, I think, to have these two sheets be tabs one and two in the same worksheet, with the "Orchestra/Performing Arts Organizations Database" as tab three. This is only a suggestion, of course; if it makes sense to you to organize these differently, you should do what serves your workflow best.

4 In my opinion, listing people you work with at Pay-to-Sings as representing the companies they work for year-round is not a particularly helpful practice, unless (1) they serve a formal casting function at that company and (2) you were heard in a setting—like a "house audition"—that was explicitly put forward as an audition and they participated *in their capacity as a casting representative* of their company. I hope the reason is obvious, but if not, it is because this practice obfuscates their function and their potential influence on your future. See chapter on YAPs for a more detailed discussion of the potential influence of various people you meet along the way.

5 You can and should monitor news about the artistic staff of (especially American) opera houses to the best of your ability so that you can maintain a clear picture of which organizations are likely to favor you for future work. Though you can often learn this information from your friends and colleagues who work in the industry, there are a couple of good web-based resources listed in the "Bookmarks" section at the end of this chapter that can help keep you current. These include Musical America, Operabase, and the *Deutsches Bühnen-Jahrbuch*.

6 You can find this information in the American Guild of Musical Artists' (AGMA) Schedule C, which is accessible by the public and can be used to determine the size (and corresponding pay scale) of various roles in all

standard (and much non-standard) repertoire. I have Schedule C open in a browser tab on my phone all the time, because I use it constantly.
7   I know that not every singer will need every part of this process in order to place themselves correctly; this is a tool to help singers who may not have access to intel to help them make these decisions.
8   So much of being strategic in anything comes down to putting yourself in the position and head space of the "end user." And while it can be difficult to imagine what the Artistic Administrator at the Metropolitan Opera is looking for if you have never talked to them, you can make good progress asking clear questions and answering them as though you were in a hiring position. "What do I need?" (A: "36 Young Artists who can handle a grueling summer of singing challenging music in our productions and high-profile concerts.") "How do I know if they can handle that workload?" (A: "Have any of them done something similar in another YAP or at a big school I'm familiar with? If yes, put them in the pile.") And so on ...

My entire approach to research can be boiled down to this: *Keep asking questions (or the same question, like "why?") until you reach a solid answer or absurdity.* I don't think it's enough to know that top-tier YAPs tend to select participants from top-tier schools; that sets up a comforting tautology (i.e. "the elite ones take the elite ones because they're elite, and that's how they stay elite"), but I have met too many of the people making those decisions to believe they would stake the reputation of their institutions on such simplistic philosophies.

And keep in mind that this process of inquiry, which answers the question, "what is?" is separate from any value judgment we might make, which answers the question, "what should be?" There is a time for both, just as there is a time for writing and for editing. *Why/what* something is has consequences to our strategic thinking; *whether* something should be is more complicated and outside the scope of this inquiry.

9   In order to save yourself money and some potential heartache, be as honest as you can about your experience vis-à-vis your colleagues in these programs. Singing Mozart's Susanna in your church basement with piano is not the same as singing it on stage with orchestra at a top graduate program or Pay-to-Sing. This is the time for brutal honesty, so look at your qualifications as objectively as you can. You'll thank yourself later.

Part III
The Nuts and Bolts of Booking Work

8 Professional Documents

In this business, it is almost guaranteed that the first encounter a casting director has with you will be through your website, where they will scan your résumé, bio, and reviews before heading over to your video and audio clips. That casting director will have a mock-up of you in mind in a matter of perhaps four to five minutes before you've ever sung a note in the same room as them, and your getting an audition will depend in no small part on whether your package presents you as a person with appropriate experience, and on the appropriate trajectory for a given opportunity. With that in mind, the next two chapters are geared toward making your materials professional and polished, and getting you in the door for auditions—instead of placed in the "Hear in Two Years" pile.

What are Professional Documents in a Singer's World?

A singer should have at least three professional documents, designed with care, updated, and ready to send out at any moment: the résumé, the biography, and the press kit. Before we dive into detailed analysis, let's look at each of them and the unique purposes they serve.

Résumé

The résumé is the clearest professional summary you give—a list of every role (or the most recent ones) or concert you have sung alongside your education and training. It features no prose, no explanation, just brute facts.

Biography

Your biography is where people learn about you as a person, you as an artist, and learn the context for all those lines on your résumé. It is an opportunity to set yourself apart from other singers, to craft a narrative that serves your artistic goals, and to make a lasting impression.

Press Kit

A basic press kit comprises four elements: head shot, biography, résumé, and reviews; it is essentially a basic website on paper. Many agents assemble these for their artists and use them in place of a simple résumé in auditions and in communications with presenting organizations.

Repertoire List

A singer should also have an exhaustive, up-to-date repertoire list in case the opportunity should arise to participate in a recital series or even orchestra concert where the repertoire is flexible. Like an academic CV (*curriculum vitae*), it is painful to assemble the first time, but once the format is set, it is very easy to update.

Basics: The Résumé[1]

Later in this chapter, we'll discuss tailoring the résumé to various audiences, but first, let's talk about what résumés have in common at all levels and contexts.

- Name—Your name should be the clearest, most visible information on the page. Use your biggest, boldest font.
- Voice type—Notice I don't say "*fach*." Just put your voice type; your résumé and audition will tell them what repertoire you sing.
- Contact information—If unmanaged, your email, phone, and website URL. If managed, your manager's email and phone and *your* website URL.
- Performance experience—Your experience is listed in two to four categories, including Roles Performed, Concert Work, and possibly Partial Roles/Scenes and/or Roles Coached (though the latter is rightfully *very* rare).
- Education and Training—This includes all[2] post-secondary degree and diploma programs, Pay-to-Sings, and YAPs.

Optional Information: The Résumé

- Headshot thumbnail—Especially when the artist isn't presenting a press kit, many choose to include a small copy of their head

shot in the upper right or left corner of their résumé, opposite their name.
- Special skills—If you have had years of formal dance training; dialect or special dramatic training (e.g. Shakespearean); stage fighting; juggling/aerial/stilt-walking or any other training that might be of interest to a director, you may want to list it here. One never knows if a director has been itching to do a circus-themed tango show set during one of the Desmond Rebellions.
- Languages—It is less common to list these on résumés as you get older, but they may help show well-roundedness for graduate school, Pay-to-Sings, or YAPs. They may also be helpful if a company is presenting an opera in a rarer language (like Czech) and you happen to have studied it formally.
- Competitions—Barring a major competition win this category should fall off of a singer's résumé by the time they sing in their first or second YAP.
- Ensemble experience—Only useful when applying for graduate school or Pay-to-Sings when your résumé is otherwise thin.
- References—To the untrained eye, this may look like a harmless name-dropping section with categories like, "Teachers," "Coaches," "Directors," "Conductors," and "Master Classes." This is *not* a name-dropping section—you are putting these people forward as references to the quality of your work. So consider the following:

Teachers: Include your regular teachers and anyone you worked with more than three or four times at a summer program.
Coaches: List coaches with whom you've worked regularly or very recently for several sessions.
Stage Directors: List directors from professional engagements and training programs only if you played a principal role.
Conductors: Unless you played a principal role, skip conductors.
Master Classes: Unless you participated in Joyce DiDonato's Carnegie Hall master class broadcast on *medici.tv*, do not list master classes. Due to the brevity and setting of your work together, these are not reliable references.

The point to remember in evaluating these references is how reliable they would be based on how much or how recently you worked with them. Put yourself on the other side of the table for a moment: a singer has listed a director from a production for which there is no corresponding role entry on the résumé. What are the options? The only option that makes sense is that the singer was in the chorus, and the director likely had no direct interaction with that singer. Do you, the administrator, even call or email to check for a reference? Of course not. So don't list it.

Reevaluate these entries every year to be sure you believe they would remember you and act as a positive reference.

Basic Principle: Dress for the Job You Want

In my private work with students I have seen scores of résumés—most of which presented these singers as precisely what they were: students. When you're applying for graduate school, there is nothing wrong with presenting as a student; but when you're applying for professional and preprofessional opportunities, you want to present as a young/emerging professional. Straightforward, right? So how do we tailor materials to the opportunity?

First and most importantly, you must consider your audience—what they're looking for, who they represent, who else they're looking at.

University Faculty Evaluating Graduate School Candidates

- Suitability for environment
- Sound technique
- Viability at next level (academic or performance)
- Academic achievement appropriate for institution.

Opera Education Director Evaluating YAP Candidates

- Solo experience appropriate for a training program and *comprimario* main stage work
- Engaging stage presence suitable for school (if that's a program component) and donor engagement, and concerts. (Young Artists are ambassadors for a company for months at a time. Companies need to know they can trust you.)

Opera Artistic Director Evaluating Main Stage Artists

- Emphasis on solo experience at an appropriate level (tier)
- Professionalism in everything
- Complete artistry.

Not everything listed above can be determined from the résumé, which is all the more reason to ensure that you effectively communicate that which can be communicated in that medium. You will prove the rest in your audition.

Basics: The Biography

Your biography gives context to your résumé, provides a narrative for your career, and allows you to bring your artistry and your persona to life. Before getting into guidelines, let's talk about where you might use a biography and what that says about length and format.

1. Website—This is your space and your chance to tell your ideal story, so this is also your longest biography: 500 words and up is no problem here.
2. Press kit—This biography is what the artistic staff may scan while they listen to you sing your first aria. It should have the repertoire/company/YAP highlights and maybe one or two well-crafted phrases—or especially good reviews—that linger in their minds. Keep this one around 250–300 words if possible. It must fit on one page.
3. Production program/company website—The company will specify their limits; have 100- and 200-word versions ready that can be massaged 25 words in either direction, just in case.
4. Social media—On Facebook, you will use some version of your website biography. On Instagram and Twitter, though, you are very limited, so try to be clever and concise. Figure out how to best tell your story in, say, 15 words.

Rebecca Davis, whose PR firm represents some of classical music's biggest stars, recommends having two different biographies for two different audiences:

> The long lists of companies and festivals and roles serve a purpose: artistic administrators read them to get a sense of your career progression. But those bios do not necessarily engage the audience in the theater.

She says that artists should consider having a second, more engaging bio to send in for programs and company websites, one that tells the audience about the artist and helps them become invested in specific singers.

The bottom line? Have fun writing your biography so that we have fun reading it. Tell the story you wish everyone could know when they hear you sing. "Tell us not just where and what you have sung but why do you sing and what made you fall in love with opera," says Davis.

Tell us in a way that is distinctly you, but for best results, be careful to avoid two common pitfalls …

The Two Inviolable Rules of Biographies

Biographies may be funny (see the late, great Bob Orth's "Dark Bio"), serious, boring (see German bios and take note if you plan to audition there), clever, or they may take any number of other approaches. But there is one thing they must *not* be: hyperbolic.

We have all seen these biographies—and may have perhaps written one for ourselves once (myself included)—and they are in every case terrible. You know the ones: loaded with clichés without citations, self-aggrandizing, utterly tone deaf to the greater opera world around them. Clichés like

> "Already being hailed ..."
> "Equally at home in [repertoire] and [repertoire] ..."
> "A champion of new works ..."
> "... one of the most sought-after tenors of his generation."

What we are after in our materials is twofold: *professionalism* and *concision*. As the French writer Antoine de Saint-Exupéry said, "Perfection is achieved not when there is nothing more to add, but when there is nothing left to take away." With that in mind:

Rule #1: If half of singers can make a claim, it is redundant to include it in your biography. (Almost every singer "feels equally at home" on the concert stage and the opera stage. And most singers are, rightfully, "champions" of new works—the rest *should* be.)

If it is redundant, it is not concise; if it is not concise, it is not professional.

Rule #2: *Do not* make any qualitative statement about yourself unless it is told through a direct, cited quote from a (preferably reputable) published review. "Already being hailed?" By whom? "Thrilling/imposing/charming/virtuosic?" Who said it, and in what context?

The proof of the pudding is in the eating: read a biography of a young singer you don't know personally. What is your reaction when you see these phrases? Do you take them at their word? Or do you say to yourself, "Who does this person think they are?"

Davis says that Young Artists should stick to their strengths in their bios, and not try to appear to be something they are not yet:

> [Younger artists] may want to use a hybrid bio. In the first paragraph, I like to lead with press quotes; if they don't have any, keep that paragraph short and move on to what they are doing now, what they have done in the past.

And, she says, don't be afraid to close with some artistic philosophy or something that brings you to life for the reader. Above all, be authentic. We want to know *who you are* as an artist and what sets you apart.

As artists, we are expected to keep up and evolve not just in our art, but to maintain a professional presence in the online world, as well. We will cover this in greater depth in Chapter 9, but Davis gives a crucial reminder to all artists: "Really invest the time in writing yourself or invest the money in hiring someone skilled to write something that really describes your artistry and point of view." Artists need to recognize, she says, that we are not always the best equipped to tell our stories, and if writing isn't a strength, we need to find someone strong in that area. Our careers are certainly worth it.

Once you have a good, professional biography, you can update it occasionally to reflect your most recent work, but you can't move things around indefinitely, Davis says. "Every few years, you have to completely rework your bio." And why not? Every few years you may be a brand-new artist, and that artist deserves to be fully represented, not tied awkwardly to a past version of themselves.

Basics: The Press Kit

As I mentioned at the beginning of the chapter, the press kit is a document that combines several other documents and acts as a miniature website for you, the artist.

I recommend the following order, which I believe is universal:

1. bio with headshot
2. résumé
3. reviews.

Staple that together with the first page in full color and hand it to the company's staff in place of a simple résumé when you arrive for your audition.

Excerpting Reviews

An artist's website should reflect all of their positive reviews and their press kit should feature as many as can fit on one or two pages. In order to make sure you always have the most up-to-date reviews:

1. Set up Google alerts for
   a. "[your name] + opera"
   b. "[your name] + [your voice type]"

84 The Nuts and Bolts of Booking Work

    c "[your name] + [voice type reviewers sometimes think you are]"
    d "[your name] + [company you worked for]"
    e "[your name] + [production you sang]," and
    f "[your name] + [role you sang]," and
    g any other useful combination you can imagine.
2 Set up a document (a Google Doc or Sheet works great) with a section for every production you have been in.[3]
3 As those Google alerts come in, write down:[4]
    a The publication name
    b The reviewer's name
    c The URL of the review
    d The relevant section (i.e. the one with your name in it) in full.

In order to keep your review page and sheet focused on relevant information, an artist must learn to excerpt the relevant information to keep the quote focused on themselves. Occasionally, a reviewer will group two or more singers together; use your discretion to determine whether the group review is demonstrative of your work, and whether the relevant line can be extracted without ruining the passage.

If your name and the quote about you are separated by other, unrelated text, it is perfectly fine to replace the pronoun that refers to you with its antecedent (your name) in the following way:

> Thomas Tenor and Suzie Soprano were magnificently paired: her coloratura seemed to float on air in one moment and engage in Cirque du Soleil-style acrobatics the next; his stentorian voice filled this theater and the one across the street and made grown men weep audibly, even in the recits.

becomes:

> [Tenor's] stentorian voice filled this theater and the one across the street and made grown men weep audibly, even in the recits.

The Repertoire List

These documents can be difficult to assemble, not least of all due to the many categories of repertoire some singers perform. This list should include everything you have studied and performed in the following categories (I note below how I organize them on my own list; you may prefer another scheme):

- Art Songs (language, then composer)
- Opera & Operetta Roles & Scenes (language, then composer)
- Opera & Operetta Arias (language, then composer)
- Oratorio Roles (by composer)
- Oratorio Arias (by composer)
- Musical Theater Roles & Scenes (by composer)
- Musical Theater songs (by composer)
- Great American Songbook (by composer).

Depending on the venue, it may make sense to remove certain sections before sending your list out, but it is always good practice to start with the most complete information possible and pare it down rather than to do the opposite.

Extra Credit: The Prospectus

This is a document I created for myself when I was looking for new management, and on which I received very positive feedback, so I want to share it with you so you can determine if it is a tool you want to use when the time comes to reach out to managers.

It is essentially a press kit on steroids: a complete rundown of who you are, what you do, what you're planning to do, and how you're planning to get there, laid out in full color, spiral bound, with a glossy cover.

Here is what mine includes:

- A *cover* (w/headshot, name/voice type/contact information—essentially a résumé header with a larger head shot);
- My *long-form biography* interspersed with three full-color production photos with contrasting characters;
- My *repertoire list for that day's audition* customized with the name of the agency and date, and seven arias instead of five, because we're building something here;
- My *résumé*, in full;
- A *complete (or nearly complete) repertoire list*, including operatic roles and arias, musical theater roles and songs, and concert repertoire. This page also includes some projected repertoire over defined periods of time. It's a bold move to call your shot in that way in front of an agent, but I was in my 30s and knew some things about my voice that a younger person in the same situation might not;
- A list of *career-related changes* for the near future: audition repertoire changes, plans to audition in Europe, and roles I plan to add to my résumé via coaching or performance soon;

- A *page of review highlights* interspersed with three more full-color production photos of contrasting characters (show your range!);
- A *discussion of a project I was working on* that wasn't necessarily something they would interact with, but which showed me to be a well-rounded person who thought seriously about his career.

You may wonder what the point of all of this was.

In Chapter 3, I told you your manager is a business partner. Chapters 7 and 10 talk about how to understand yourself as a product and build your singing business around that product. This prospectus? It is exactly what you would put together for a potential business partner or investor in any other industry: a 360-degree view of the business you want to build with them. And it really does have a limited audience (agents); this information, including future/aspirational ideas is not meant for public consumption.

When I sang for agents, I rented the room, set up their table and chairs, and placed one copy of the prospectus on the table in front of each chair before they arrived (or handed it to them if they had already set up the room). While I sang, I watched them read, make notes, and at the end, in all but one case, we had a long and detailed conversation about the material in the prospectus.

Each copy cost about $2.50 to print, and the entire project took about 3 hours to design from scratch in Adobe InDesign. And it had the desired effect: serious conversations with serious people who, whether we became partners or not, left with the impression that I was someone who thought clearly about my future and my business. And they left with an eight-page physical document they could re-read on the way back to the office if the Internet cut out on the train!

You will come to learn that those interactions are rare and more valuable than you realize at the time, so I encourage you to consider investing in your business in a similar way when the time comes. Perhaps you won't have the opportunity to sit with agents in the same way, and so a prospectus may be too much—but you will never regret undertaking the time and/or expense necessary to make sure that every piece of your brand that people interact with looks polished and professional. In a world where first impressions matter *and* we can't control which format our first impression takes (whether audition, website, Instagram, or YouTube video), it is worthwhile to convey professionalism in every possible venue. After all, no casting director or employer ever complained that someone was too professional for the job.

Summary of Key Principles

1 *Your documents represent you not just in content, but in presentation.* They begin to answer the question, "Is this person a professional?" before you ever open your mouth. Take pride in them and invest in them when appropriate.
2 *If you are not a gifted writer, find someone who is to write your bio.* Artists work too hard to be undermined by poor copy speaking for them. It is not as expensive as you think to hire a very good writer who is familiar with the format.
3 *Your résumé should quickly tell your audience you are qualified for the job.* From content to formatting, it has only a few seconds to communicate your preparedness, so it must be up to standard.
4 *Your bio should tell the entire story you want to tell in the fewest possible words.* Remember: if it isn't concise, it isn't professional.
5 *When the time comes to write a professional bio, look at the bios of famous artists you admire.* Emulate the bios of your heroes, not your fellow Young Artists.

Application Questions

1 If I am casting a show, what does this (my) résumé tell me about this singer's:
   a Experience/preparedness?
   b Professionalism?
   c Repertoire and trajectory?
2 Am I presenting myself as a professional, an emerging professional, or an amateur?
3 How can I present this information so that it highlights my most relevant experience and shows both professionalism and readiness for opportunities?
4 Is there any information on my résumé that is outdated or inappropriate for this opportunity?
5 Is my biography free from clichés, un-cited self-aggrandizement, and boring blocks of company names?

Bookmarks

- Bob Orth's "Dark Bio," archived (accessed 15 August 2019) (web.archive.org/web/20190311030943/www.robertorth.com:80/darkbio.htm)
- Rebecca Davis PR (www.rebeccadavispr.com)

88 *The Nuts and Bolts of Booking Work*

- "YAP Bootcamp: Résumés" (www.operacareers.com/2018/12/22/YAP-Bootcamp-Resumes)
- If This, Then That (www.IFTTT.com)

Build Your Business

1. Make a list of all your performance experience, education/training, honors/awards (including competition wins), and references.
2. Build a new résumé from scratch, using the order prescribed above, and listing experience in reverse chronological order within sections.
3. Print this new résumé out and see whether it looks cluttered or otherwise awkward to the eye.
4. Create a PDF of this résumé and upload both the PDF and .DOC file to your cloud-based storage.
5. Upload the PDF to your YAP Tracker profile and delete old résumés. Determine whether you have need of a separate résumé for other types of opportunities. If so, repeat the process.
6. Find an experienced writer to write your biography (~500 words, ~250 words, ~100 words, and ~50 words). Place it on your website and in your press kit. Place downloadable PDFs of your résumé, bio, and press kit on your website so people may access them without asking.

Notes

1. I am consciously abstaining from giving examples of actual résumés because I don't want to dictate formatting or any other element of presentation. There are plenty of examples online if you are interested, and most are boring as sin. I am hopeful that résumés in opera will undergo a bit of a design renaissance soon so that multitalented singers can communicate more of their unique skill sets and artistry through that document.
2. There is (still, somehow) a persistent bias in the opera world against doctoral degrees that essentially says that if a person is pursuing a doctorate, they are no longer serious about singing. This is demonstrably false, but the bias persists, nonetheless. Since you are trying to book auditions and engagements and have no way of knowing who holds this bias, I advise you to leave D.M.A. and Ph.D. studies off of your performance résumé. Of course, if someone really wants to know if you are working on a doctorate, they will find out, but it is prudent, I think, not to hand them this information without knowing how they see it.
3. Perhaps it goes without saying, but every document that you create should be mirrored somewhere online (in the cloud) for easy access. Creating these documents in Google Suite or Microsoft Office 365/OneDrive, for

example, means you don't have to go to any extra effort to ensure that it is accessible anywhere you go, or if your hard drive should fail, as hard drives sometimes do.
4 There is a web service I recommend called "If This, Then That" (www.IFTTT.com) through which you can use your Google alerts RSS feed to automatically populate a Google Doc or Sheet with some of this information, which you can supplement later with full text, and so on. It is worth looking into.

Reference

Rebecca Davis, phone conversation with the author, August 16, 2019.

9 Cultivating Your Online Presence

As singers, we present ourselves publicly and professionally in a variety of ways: on stage, where we work; at donor and other VIP functions, where we network; and not least of all, on the Internet. While singers 40 years ago could allow the press and their managers to publicize them, today's singers have to be savvy self-promoters in addition to skilled performers. And while it would be nice not to have to worry about anything but the work of singing, I believe that not only is it important from a personal business standpoint, but that well-executed online strategies (even if the singers themselves wouldn't call it something so stiff) are a potentially transformational tool for singers and the industry at large for the foreseeable future.

Step One: Your Website

As a singer, you absolutely must have a website. This is the primary place people will look for you to find upcoming events, learn about you if they are seeing you in a show, and evaluate you for opportunities. In short, it is the most important outward-facing aspect of your business after yourself, so I advise you to take the time necessary to ensure that everything about your site—from color scheme to URL (domain) to media files—reflects how you want people to see you professionally.

Format

A good basic website will have four to five pages:

- Home—the first thing people see when they come to your page. For some singers, it is as simple as a solid color background, their name, and their head shot or a compelling production photo.

Others choose to feature more information on the front page, including upcoming events/news or their bio.
- About—this page typically features a secondary photo (alternate head shot or production photo) or two alongside the full-length biography. It is good practice to note the date of the bio's most recent revision in parentheses—that is, "(Revised MM/YY)"—at the end so visitors know how recent the information is. At the end of the bio, include links to downloadable PDFs of your biography in various lengths: 500+ word, 250, 150, and 75, for example. These may all be in one document, for simplicity's sake.
- Schedule—include all of your upcoming performances in a readable format of your choosing. Information may include date/time, company name, opera, role, ticketing link, company's promotional artwork for the production.
- Media—include recent high-quality audio and video, as well as photos—both promotional (head shots, full-body shots, "lifestyle" shots) and production photos provided by organizations with whom you've performed.
- Contact—this page is simple to design (every plug-and-play website building service has a contact form) and may include any combination of your contact information and that of your management team(s). If you provide multiple points of contact (yourself, your American agent, your European agent), be sure to state clearly which person should be contacted under which circumstances.

Hosting

If you are a beginner at web design, I suggest using one of the main "drag-and-drop" web builders: Wix, Squarespace, or Weebly. These services offer attractive templates and built-in hosting plans ($15–25/month) that typically include a free one-year domain registration. They also offer the option of adding on email and analytics services, though I recommend doing this separately through Google so that your email service stays operable in the event that you change hosting services at some point.

The Master of Your Domain

You may choose to use your full name, your full name and voice type, some other version of your name, or a clever brand under which you plan to establish yourself, but there is one rule you absolutely must follow: *make it as simple as possible.*

To illustrate this point, picture yourself at a crowded and noisy industry function: the din of the crowd, clinking glasses and bottles, and amid all of it, you happen to meet the artistic director of a very interesting company or project. You speak briefly and make a connection, and just as this VIP gets pulled away from you and other bodies begin to fill the space between you, they ask for your website or email. Let's imagine your name is Kristopher Anderssen, and you're a tenor. Now, in communicating your name to someone,[1] you already must explain the two variations between the spelling of your name and the traditional English spellings of each part. In the best-case scenario, you have chosen something like the following as your URL:

- Kristopheranderssen.com
- Kristopher-Anderssen.com
- KAtenor.com
- Anderssentenor.com

Each is easily communicated and easily "Google-able" if someone knows a small bit of information about you.

Now imagine the difficulty you might have in the same scenario communicating the following URL to someone under the same conditions:
KristopherJakobAnderssen-Tenor.net
"It's Kristopher, with a 'K,' Jakob, with a 'k,' Anderssen, but '-s, s, e, n' instead of '-s, o, n' … DASH, tenor, dot NET!"
The moment has passed. And while this scene is perhaps exaggerated, it is not outrageous. Unnecessary complexity will hinder your message. My advice is to find the simplest expression of your identity or brand that you can buy under ".com" and build your site there. It will save you headaches later.

Step Two: Social Media

When I asked Melinda Massie, a performing arts social media specialist, if all aspiring singers should be on social media, she was emphatic. "*Yes*," she said. "You don't have to be on every platform, but you have to be out there, and consistent enough that we know you still exist." International baritone Lucas Meachem, who runs the popular *Baritone Blog*, agreed, "We're witnessing a huge change in the way artists interact with their fans and it's exciting." But, he says, "If artists aren't on social media, they're just left out of the cut." Asked frankly about their interaction with artists' social media channels, many artistic staffers at American opera houses admit that though it doesn't necessarily influence casting decisions, they do pay attention to artists' social media accounts to some extent.

So what is an aspiring singer to do?

Developing a social media plan is like developing your career plan: it helps to start with the end in mind. If you are going to put in the effort to build an engaging social media presence, what benefit are you hoping to derive from it? The answer, in simplest possible terms: engagement. Explains Massie, "Whichever platforms you choose to invest in, you want everything you do to point back to your website." Why? "You want to *own* your main presence on the Internet, which you do with your website." Meachem also prioritizes engagement, though in different terms:

> [T]he connections online are what make each post worth it. I put a lot of time and thought into my blog and social media posts, and to receive in return comments and messages from opera lovers around the world is what it's all for.

Telling Stories

"What I share is based on what I think my followers want to see. I share my journey *to* success, not *of* success. My social media strategy is to serve others, not myself," says Meachem, who also uses social media to keep tabs on his friends and colleagues in the industry.

Platforms

While it can be overwhelming to build your online presence from scratch, an artist can effectively tailor their "mix" to their business goals or their strengths and interests. The major platforms (Facebook, Instagram, Twitter) function differently, have different audiences, and have their own strengths and weaknesses that can inform an artist's strategy.

"*Facebook*'s strength is *sheer numbers*," says Massie. "It's the platform with the largest number of users and the broadest demographic cross-section among its usership, so if you want to get a message out, Facebook is the place to start." She also favors Facebook for the ability to create and share events, which provides a means for "getting on to people's calendars" that is lacking in the other platforms.

Instagram's strength is in its simplicity and reliance upon visual impact, she says, which provides opportunities to deliver unique behind-the-scenes content and tell a different type of story about a singer. According to her analytics, Instagram also drives the most engaged visitors to her website. As both a consumer and an artist, Meachem favors it for the ease with which it delivers its message. "Instagram is a favorite of mine because it's basically a visual diary of my day-to-day life. It's easier and quicker to post there and we're all in it for information and inspiration."

> I swipe over to Instagram to get the latest news on what's happening in the classical music world. I see album releases, tour schedules, concert announcements, and all the behind-the-scenes action or pictures that never make it to publication, making it more personalized than [other media].

"*Twitter* is the cocktail party to Facebook's dinner party," says Massie. She considers Twitter an excellent networking resource but finds the conversational nature of the platform ineffective for broadcasting messages. "The conversation moves so fast on Twitter it's hard to know who you've reached." Still, she finds the networking possibilities very valuable, and has occasionally connected with future customers and collaborators there.

Analytics and End Games

Once you have put the time and effort into building an engaging online presence, how do you know whether it is achieving the goals you intended to achieve? The simple answer is to collect data and analyze them. For example, one very easy form of analysis can help guide the kind of content you create on various platforms: keep track of the number of "likes" and comments that certain posts of yours get and create more of that kind of post. This is similar to Lucas Meachem's approach, outlined above.

But recall also that the goal of social media from a business perspective is to *drive your audience to your website*. Web analytics[2] is a powerful tool to help you understand the behaviors of your audience and the quality (from a business perspective) of your interactions with them.

Scheduling and Automating Your Social Media

If you're like me, you may find the thought of directing, producing, and executing a robust social media strategy exhausting, and wonder how you will find time to attend to the singing aspect of your career among all of these new responsibilities.

You Gotta Get a Gimmick if You Wanna Get Ahead

There's a Stephen Sondheim quote for everything, I think. In this case, the advice he offers in *Gypsy* isn't entirely true, though it is undeniably potent if well-executed. Many opera singers have found their own "hooks," so to speak, and have won appreciative followings on social media and in real life as a result. Some examples of effective recurring features on some singers' channels include:

- Opera Cowgirls—a creation of mezzo-soprano Caitlin McKechney, the lineup of this country-meets-opera cover band has included several working opera singers over the years, all of whom play instruments in the band. In addition to its online videos, the band plays shows in New York and other cities across the U.S.
- #LindsayPlaysUkulele—Soprano Lindsay Ohse has been creating videos of herself singing arias from current and upcoming engagements while accompanying herself on ukulele. Lately, she has taken to including some of her cast mates, as in recent videos from the Metropolitan Opera's production of *Akhnaten* and *Cendrillon* at Opera Middlebury.
- Blythely Oratonio—As if Stephanie Blythe needed a gimmick! The world-famous diva's creativity simply can't be contained even by the world's biggest opera stages, so in one of the greatest moments in the history of opera, she created a drag persona, Blythely Oratonio, and performed an original song called "Martha" (including part of the aria "M'appari" from Flotow's *Martha*) in a Philadelphia cabaret with local drag queen "Martha Graham Cracker."
- Will Liverman's videos—In addition to being a world-class baritone, Will Liverman is an outstanding pianist who has carved out a bit of a cult following for his hilarious videos featuring his impressions of opera characters accompanied by gospel music, takes on child discipline and professionalism in opera, and general backstage antics.
- Other non-opera music pursuits—Many singers who do most of their work in the opera world take to Instagram and Facebook to share non-operatic musical pursuits, running the gamut from art song to original electronic music and beyond. Not only is it a much-needed change of pace for professionals who work in a demanding field, but it's an effective way for audience members past, present, and future to connect with us as humans, and that is a powerful way for people to build lasting attachments to what we do.

- The #OperaBard—Soprano Kelli Butler combined her identity as an operatic soprano with her love of *Dungeons & Dragons* and created the "College of the Opera"—a subclass of bards whose skills include speaking four languages and a "Shatter" spell. As the character levels up, they can further equip themselves with their choice of three arias that boost their abilities in different ways. I have no way of knowing what the overlap between opera fans and *Dungeons & Dragons* fans is, but I think this is an amazing example of expanding our reach through our non-operatic interests.
- Other non-music hobbies—In addition to being world travelers as part of their jobs, several opera singers I know are photographers of various sorts (travel, portrait, live music, wedding) and their Instagrams are some of the most awe-inspiring and inspirational in my feed.

Can Social Media Save the (Opera) World?

Building a thoughtful, consistent online presence can seem like an overwhelming or hopelessly vague thing, but it needn't be tedious or forced. A singer's online presence, especially social media, presents them with a powerful channel for creating meaningful connections with people—both in our audiences and beyond. At a time when some journalists can't resist the urge to sound opera's death knell, established and rising professionals in the industry are using their social media to share parts of themselves and their lives that audiences don't get to see on stage, and building powerful connections in the process. It is not outlandish to think that these efforts have already inspired people to buy their first ticket or take their first voice lesson, to don their first cape or Viking helmet, or look up their first aria on some online music platform. In a world of data-driven advertising and focus group-approved experiences, it may well be that opera's audience of the future is just waiting to make an authentic connection to something real, visceral, and new. What an opportunity we have before us if we can seize it.

Summary of Key Principles

1 *Singers eschew building an online presence at their peril.* At bare minimum, singers should own their personal domain and should have an attractive website with a photo, biography, recordings, schedule, and contact information.
2 *If you're going to get into the social media game (and most should, to some extent), do so strategically.* Play to your strengths: if you

don't like to tell stories visually, Instagram may not be for you. If you have events going to promote, you should be on Facebook. You don't have to be present on all platforms to be effective; in fact, if you're apprehensive about one medium or another, stay away—a poorly executed online presence can be worse for you than none at all.

3 *Tracking your engagement through analytics is a powerful way to learn about your audience—and give them more of what they want.* Activate analytics on your website's dashboard and learn how most people find your website, what they look at, and how long they stay. Make a spreadsheet of your social media posts to track engagement. What kinds of posts get the most likes? The most comments?

Application Questions

1 What is the story I am trying to tell through my online presence (website, social media)? How is that story most effectively told?
2 How comfortable am I using the various social media platforms? To what extent does each play to my strengths?
3 Is there an interest or talent of mine that I can present compellingly through my social media that may help people feel connected to and invested in me?

Bookmarks

- Melinda Massie (www.MelindaMassie.com)—Dallas-Fort Worth-based performing arts marketing coach
- Squarespace (www.Squarespace.com)—Drag-and-drop website hosting platform
- Wix (www.Wix.com)—Drag-and-drop website hosting platform
- Weebly (www.Weebly.com)—Drag-and-drop website hosting platform
- Later (www.Later.com)—Instagram post scheduler
- Hootsuite (www.Hootsuite.com)—Multi-platform social media post scheduler

Build Your Business

1 If you don't own it already, buy the most memorable personal domain name you can find and choose a hosting platform.
2 Gather your best headshots and recordings and populate a great looking template to call your online "home."

3   Activate analytics on your website's dashboard to see how people are finding you.
4   Try to build a basic seven-day social media content plan. On each day of the week, choose a category of post to share. For example:
    a   Reviews from past performances
    b   Behind-the-scenes
    c   Inspirational quotes (e.g. "#MotivationMonday")
    d   Family/pets feature ("#FamilyFriday?")
    e   Production photos
    f   #WorkoutWednesday, if that's your thing.
    Don't feel as though you have to post every day or share all of these kinds of material, but consider these as guidelines for building a diverse backlog of posts that can be scheduled throughout the week or month with minimal effort beyond curation.

Notes

1   Of course, you can always mitigate this risk to some extent by carrying business cards, but I think that objectively, people tend to find long URLs clunky, amateurish, and a bit of a hassle. In branding yourself or any endeavor you undertake (e.g. concert series, book titles, ensembles), consider how easy or difficult it will be for two strangers to pass along your information in conversation. Word-of-mouth marketing is powerful and free, so it behooves us to make it as easy as possible for people to talk about us.
2   Google is the main provider of these services, it seems, and their tools may be integrated with most web hosting platforms.

References

Melinda Massie, phone conversation with the author, August 15, 2019.
Lucas Meachem, email to the author, August 25, 2019.

10 You, Inc. (Building Your Business)

As a professional singer, you are self-employed. A small business owner. Chairman and CEO of "You, Inc.": an organization that thrives and struggles in proportion to your success as both artist and entrepreneur. As such, you must learn to think as much about the financial, marketing, and other business aspects of your career as you do about the artistic aspects—in both the present *and* future. This does not come naturally to most artists, and that is okay—it's why you're reading this book. So, let's begin to set up your business.

Budgeting

It is my personal opinion that everyone should work off of a written budget—I have personally experienced a written budget's power to make me feel as though I make two to three times what I actually do, and to help me reach savings goals and stay afloat while I'm on the road. Our lives often cycle through months-long stretches of feast and fallow, so it is important to learn to stretch our dollars.

Because of the often-unpredictable nature of our income, I like to write a little more detail than most into my budget, but I'll start you off with a basic sketch (see Table 10.1). This format works well for almost all households—especially those who have considerably more income than expenses in each month—with some minor tweaking. It lists all the known income and expenses you have in each month and allows you to look at your monthly finances from a big-picture standpoint.

The budget I prefer to use, regardless of the particulars of my financial situation, is what I call a "Chronological Budget" (see Table 10.2), and it works like balancing your checkbook ahead of time.

I prefer this format because I can know at a glance that a certain day or two will be lean, and that I should watch my account closely. This mitigates the anxiety that comes from lean days by allowing you

100 *The Nuts and Bolts of Booking Work*

Table 10.1 Simple Monthly Budget

Source	Date	Amount
St. Bonaventure Church	4/1	$650
Private Lessons	4/1	2,000
Bill's Music Academy	4/1	400
Metro Schools	4/9	725
Bill's Music Academy*	4/15	400
Metro Schools*	4/23	725
	Total	$4,900

Expense	Due Date	Amount
Savings	4/1	$300
Mortgage/Rent	4/1	650
Electric	4/15	125
Internet/Cable	4/25	120
Insurance	4/13	245
Groceries	4/1	400
Gas/Transportation	4/15	75
Netflix	4/9	15
Entertainment	4/1	100
Credit Card 1	4/12	250
Credit Card 2	4/19	180
Student Loan 1	4/20	350
Student Loan 2	4/20	250
Lessons	4/15	300
Dance Class	4/1	60
Website	4/4	20
	Total	$3,440

*You may prefer to combine repeat deposits into one lump sum in this format.

to expect them, prepare for them, and know when and by what mechanism you will move out of them.

There are lots of great sites with budgeting resources, so I don't intend to reinvent the wheel here; excellent information on debt management and budgeting, including sample budgets, may be found at DaveRamsey.com, for one. Also, I highly recommend setting up a free account with Mint or a similar tool that can give you an up-to-date snapshot of your financial health, spending habits, and progress toward goals.

"Cashflow Deserts"

When you work with AGMA companies, you should receive a per diem when you arrive (or at contractually stipulated intervals) and may also receive either rehearsal pay or payments of a portion of

Table 10.2 Chronological Budget

Date	INCOME/Expense	Amount	Current Bal.
4/1	ST BONAVENTURE CHURCH	$650	$650
4/1	Food: 4/1–7	-120	530
4/3	American Express	-200	330
4/5	Netflix	-15	315
4/6	Citi Card	-100	215
4/7	Gas	-25	190
4/8	Food: 4/8–14	-120	70
4/9	METRO SCHOOLS	725	795
4/11	Insurance	-245	550
4/12	Student Loan	-340	210
4/15	BILL'S MUSIC ACADEMY	400	610
4/15	Food: 4/15–21	-120	490
4/15	Gas	-25	465
4/17	Electricity	-120	345
4/22	Food: 4/22–28	-120	225
4/23	METRO SCHOOLS	725	950
4/24	Internet/Cable	-115	835
4/28	Rent	-650	185
4/29	Food: 4/29–5/5	-120	65

your contract at regular intervals to sustain you through the length of the contract. When you work at non-union (non-AGMA) opera companies, you will almost never receive a per diem, and can expect to wait until the final performance for your entire fee and travel reimbursement (if applicable). This means that more often than not, for three to five weeks at a time while you work in a non-union house, you are living out-of-pocket, paying not only rent and utilities back home, but all of your food and transportation costs while you rehearse.

Budgeting will help, but if you don't have a partner who is making a regular income that enables your career, I recommend you attempt to negotiate the following terms into all your contracts:

1   company-booked travel or travel reimbursement on day one of the contract,[1]
2   a per diem or a portion (I recommend 15–20 percent, depending on the fee and contract length) of the contract paid up front to cover living expenses,[2]
3   optional: a portion of the contract fee paid out at the midway point of the contract.[3]

Though these points won't change the total financial impact of your contracted fee, they may help to mitigate the financial difficulties that can befall younger artists at the regional level by allowing them to budget, eat, and pay their bills without resorting to extreme measures to counteract their dwindling bank accounts while they wait for closing night.

Income and Expenses

As a business owner, you can expect to undertake business expenses, and depending on your business structure, many of those may or may not be deductible from your tax burden.

This is an area in which much bad advice floats around, and bad tax advice is very dangerous. "Deductions" refer to expenses you incur that may be subtracted from your total taxable income in a given year, reducing your tax liability. It is important to understand that these are not subtracted from your taxes, but your taxable income, and as such, expenses you incur are not deductible in a 1:1 ratio from your total tax liability.

Table 10.3 contains a list of common expenses that you may take as deductions on your taxes.[4] This list is subject to change—check with your certified tax preparer.

Side Jobs

Unless you're one of the lucky few who catapult to stardom out of the gate, you're going to need a side job (or a series of them) to pay your rent between gigs. Most singers I know do some combination of teaching (either music lessons or substitute teaching in larger

Table 10.3 Deductible Expenses

May Deduct	May Not Deduct
• Travel for auditions/jobs	• Gym memberships
• Theater tickets (research, incl. tix for agents, directors)	• Clothing (except uniforms, costumes)
• Out-of-town meals/meals with business contacts	• Tuxedos/gowns (a tuxedo is not a uniform)
• ~30–50% of personal cell phone bill	• Monthly metro cards in home city
• ~30–50% of personal Internet bill	• Haircuts/styling and hair care products
• Voice lessons	• Tablets/laptops
• Certain lessons/classes	
• Professional website hosting	

metropolitan areas), church gigs, and temporary ("temp") office work. Many others wait tables, or have side businesses that they run, including consulting, coaching, providing services (like web design, photography, accounting, financial advising), or network sales (think products like Arbonne, Younique, and Lularoe). Regardless of what you choose to do, you will need a job that gives you the flexibility to leave for a few weeks at a time in order to pursue performance and training opportunities.

A Note on the Pursuit of Stability

I have personally known dozens of singers who have "retired" or slowed their performing considerably because of life changes, including finding a steady job that gave them financial stability, a place to call home, and a chance to do something else at which they are skilled and challenged. I hope you will understand that there is *no shame* in this. Singing is not a moral obligation, and neither is poverty. This is a very difficult business, and the economics of it can be brutal for years at a time.

Very early in my career, I worked with a singer/voice professor who told me a story that illustrated this perfectly for me. Several years prior, she had been a part of a well-received production at the original New York City Opera. When that production moved to the Metropolitan Opera, she was contacted and offered the same role she played at City Opera—and turned it down. When I asked her why, she said, "I was happy where I was, and it was enough for me to know I *could* have sung at the Met." I was stunned, and all these years later, I am still plumbing the wisdom of her words. What I have been able to understand from it is this: none of us can know what our path to, through, and after singing will look like, but being sensitive to our changing priorities puts us on the road to contentment in whatever we choose, whether in or out of the singing world.

Taxes for the Singer[5]

Tax time is probably the scariest time of year for self-employed musicians. While most taxpayers have one or two employers who pay them, self-employed musicians may have a dozen or more sources of income each year. Keeping track of this income and the associated taxes can add up to a significant organizational and financial burden each spring, if you are not well-organized.

Since tax laws change regularly in ways large and small, and because our income and tax liabilities can change so significantly from year to year, this section will focus on a few "big-picture" considerations that may be adapted to whatever legal and tax environment singers work under in years to come.

The two main kinds of income you will encounter as a singer are:

- 1099 income—paid for freelance work, with no taxes withheld; and
- W2 income—paid by an employer, who withholds taxes on your behalf.

Broadly speaking, a singer has three options for managing their tax liability throughout the year:

1. Take the Standard Deduction[6]
2. Itemize Deductions
3. Claim Per Diem for Travel Expenses and Itemize Other Expenses.

Under this final approach, the singer keeps a log of work-related travel days to which the per diem rate (as determined by the U.S. General Services Administration, or GSA) will be applied. This deduction will cover meals and lodging while traveling for work (engagements and auditions), without requiring receipts or individual documentation. Your log will be all your accountant needs to calculate this deduction, but under an audit, your contracts, email correspondence, and travel confirmations should suffice for proof. See Table 10.4 to get an idea of what a sample travel log might look like.

Track Your Expenses

Create a spreadsheet (or use the one on my website) for tracking expenses. I recommend a system that organizes at least by month and then category (or vice versa) and associated gig/audition. There are mobile apps that can handle most of this information for a modest monthly membership fee, though they vary in the amount of metadata you can apply.

Set Money Aside for Taxes

It is important that you realize that because your 1099 income is not taxed on the front end, you're going to be responsible for paying the correct amount of self-employment tax on your own. Many singers I know do this quarterly, that is, every three months. A good rule of thumb is to set aside 25–30 percent of each paycheck into savings to pay your taxes.

Utilizing the GSA Per Diem Rate

Any time you travel for work, your food and lodging expenses are deductible, as are certain incidental expenses you incur. You should track all of these and compare them to the GSA Per Diem Rate for each city to which you traveled.

Here's how it works:

- Each year, the federal government allots a certain amount of travel-related food and lodging expenses as deductible for each city or metropolitan area in the U.S.
- This rate is broken down into a lodging amount and a "Meals and Incidental Expenses (MIE)" rate.[7]
- You may deduct from your income 50 percent of one lodging and one MIE rate per day that you spent in a given city, as long as you were there on business (for singers, this includes auditions). You do not need to keep receipts to claim this deduction, just enumerate the days spent in each city, and organize those by audition or job.
- The GSA specifies a separate rate for your travel days to/from a gig. Make a note of those in your recordkeeping.

Example: I plan an audition tour to New York City in December of 2019. I am staying for five days, with a travel day on each end. If I don't want to keep receipts, I can list this trip as in Table 10.4.

Find an Experienced Tax Preparer

Finally, if you don't trust yourself with software or an online service, *get a good tax preparer or accountant* who understands the unique

Table 10.4 Sample Travel Log

Date	City	State	Travel?	MIE	Lodging	Total	Deduct (50%)
12/2/19	NYC	NY	Y	$57	$298	$355	$177.50
12/3/19	NYC	NY	N	$76	$298	$374	$187
12/4/19	NYC	NY	N	$76	$298	$374	$187
12/5/19	NYC	NY	N	$76	$298	$374	$187
12/6/19	NYC	NY	N	$76	$298	$374	$187
12/7/19	NYC	NY	N	$76	$298	$374	$187
12/8/19	NYC	NY	Y	$57	0	$57	$28.50
			2			$2282	**$1141**

challenges we face as singers. Additionally, in many cities, there are government and non-government organizations that offer free tax preparation for families that fall under a certain income level. Search online for "free tax preparation [your city]" to see if your city has free or reduced-cost options.

Incorporating

As you grow in your career, you may find that your finances are getting more complex or you may wonder if there are tax advantages to incorporating your singing business. The main options available to singers are

- Sole proprietorship
- Limited liability company (LLC)
- Corporation ("S-Corp" or "C-Corp").

and each has its benefits and drawbacks as concerns the singer's finances, and it is worth speaking to a tax professional to determine whether your situation would benefit from forming an LLC, S-Corp, or C-Corp. Everyone who collects freelance income is by default a sole proprietorship. Under the 2017 "Tax Cuts and Jobs Act" ("TCJA") passed by the 115th United States Congress, freelancers (including singers) are limited in the kinds of expenses they can deduct during the course of W2 work in ways they are not restricted under 1099 work. However, many singers may find that their itemized deductions do not reach the threshold of the increased standard deduction and find it beneficial to claim the latter.

The benefits and drawbacks of the various arrangements can be broadly understood in terms of a few factors: taxes (who pays, and how), legal liability, and administration (i.e. paperwork and associated fees). See Table 10.5 for a comparison of the various options.

Planning for the Future

With the prospect of student loan repayment looming, not to mention expensive audition seasons, many young singers don't believe that planning for retirement is possible. Still others let the perceived complexity of investing and setting up a Roth IRA stop them from taking concrete steps toward securing their financial futures—but this thinking is allowing their present insecurity to rob them of future security. There *are* simple steps and tools available to help everyone start saving. I spoke with baritone Jeremiah Johnson to get some

Table 10.5 Legal Structure of Business

	Sole Proprietorship	Limited Liability Company (LLC)	"C" Corporation	"S" Corporation
Taxes	Profits taxed on owner's personal tax returns	• Income "passes through" to personal tax returns • Subject to 15.3% Self-Employment Tax (2019 figure) • Option to be taxed as "C" or "S" Corp instead	Income is double-taxed: • All corporate income is taxed at the prevailing corporate tax rate, then • Income paid to owner is taxed at owner's personal income tax rate	• Income "passes through" to owner's personal tax returns and is subject to 15.3% Self-Employment Tax (2019 figure) • Income that remains in the business is not subject to SI tax.
Legal/Financial Liability	Owner personally liable for all debts and legal actions against business	Only LLC is liable	Only Corp is liable	Only Corp is liable
Administration	Little to no paperwork, depending on state	Less paperwork than corporation	Expensive to form; requires extensive paperwork to form and maintain	Expensive to form; requires extensive paperwork to form and maintain

advice for singers who want to make their futures more stable than their present circumstances.

Q: *So, I want to get your thoughts on some wide-angle ideas and then we'll drill deeper. Talk to me about student loan debt for singers.*
A: First, I don't know that from a debt-to-income standpoint, going to graduate school for voice is the correct way to handle things. That's not to say you don't learn a lot, but from a return-on-investment standpoint, every person who goes to undergrad and graduate school and isn't on a full scholarship is likely to have a solid five-figure debt load. And if you're going into a field that doesn't have any kind of reasonable expectation of a steady income—and this one doesn't—it isn't a very strong choice. And if you've got a $500–1,000 per month student loan payment, how are you going to afford lessons, coachings, applications, auditions, and travel—never mind your living expenses? How are you going to make any progress in your craft when you've basically got a second rent payment every month?

Q: *Okay, so let's say I'm a young artist with $50,000 of student loan debt. There's no way I can plan for my financial future, right?*
A: My big hill to die upon in the operatic world is that *all* of us must be able to prepare for our own retirement, because apart from a tenured position in academia, you will have no retirement set up for you. You run your own business, and as a business owner, you are responsible for providing for things like health insurance and retirement for your staff—and in this case, your staff is yourself. And the good news is that the single greatest asset that Young Artists have in their arsenal is *time*. All of us can set up retirement accounts for ourselves apart from a day job, and because of compound interest, even a modest investment on a day-to-day basis—especially when you're young—can turn into a stunning amount of money.

Let's take the example of a 20-year old—a junior or senior in college, and assume they want to retire at the American average of 65. If they can put literally just $5 per day in a standard retirement account from today until they turn 65 (assuming 10 percent return, which is fairly easy to find), they will have $1.2 *million* dollars at retirement—and that is assuming that $5 per day or $150 per month is all they can ever afford to contribute. If they use more conservative strategies and get only 7 percent, they'll have $514,000. But if they wait 10 years and assume the same contribution and return, that half-million dollars turns into about $250,000. And if they don't start until they're 40, that drops to $113,000—and that's not enough to live on. So starting early really significantly changes outcomes.

Q: What is your advice for people who want to start budgeting?
A: My biggest advice is this:

1   If you are *proactive* rather than *reactive*, you put yourself in a much better position throughout the year, because suddenly, you're driving the world around you rather than reacting to it.
2   Look at your bank statements from last audition season. Figure out what it cost you to do everything you did and divide by 10–12 (depending on when your season starts) and put that amount of money aside each month in savings. Don't let audition season be one giant hit to your account. It's right around the holidays and December/January rent every year. Plan ahead.
3   There are many budgeting programs and tools out there. Budgeting is like a workout plan. It doesn't matter what plan works for me—what matters is finding a plan that you will stick to. Find one that works for you and stick to it.

Q: What are the most common misconceptions about taxes that you can help dispel for us?
A: There are so many apocryphal ideas about taxes that float around our business, and mythology left over from decades ago that I love to clear up for singers.

For one, there is no reason to keep paper receipts for anything anymore. There are apps that allow you to scan receipts and attach metadata—I use QuickBooks Self-Employed, which links to your bank account and learns your behavior and will categorize your expenses for you over time. And as a bonus, QuickBooks is owned by the same company as TurboTax, so at tax time, all your data can be moved right over there.

And if you want to keep really clean records, open a separate checking account that you only use for business.

And there is almost no scenario in which you can deduct clothing (including tuxedos and gowns).

But I think the biggest thing for people to know is that *most* singers don't need to track their expenses anymore because the standard deduction comes to more than their itemized deductions. The current [as of 2019] standard deduction is around $12,000 for single people, $24,000 for married couples filing jointly. If you're like most singers, your deductions are nowhere near that.

Stronger Together

There is perhaps no stronger or more vocal advocate for the rights of opera singers in their capacities as workers than David Salsbery Fry.

The Nuts and Bolts of Booking Work

David is a working singer who recently ran for the presidency of our labor union (AGMA) on a bold singer-centered platform, and I invited him to share his thoughts with you in this section.

From David:

> If you are dedicated and persistent, sustaining a career as an opera singer is an achievable goal. But obtaining a career that will sustain YOU is far more challenging than it ought to be. The landscape for American artists is about as difficult as it has been at any time in the last 80 years, and it is this landscape that you will be traversing as you begin building your career.
>
> Some companies will consider you an employee when you work for them, relieving you of the burden of half of your Social Security taxes, and increasing the likelihood that you will be able to file for unemployment if needed when the gig is done, but limiting the deductibility of some of the expenses you incur in pursuit of your craft. Other companies will insist on classifying you as an independent contractor, even though your work in no way resembles the paradigm of the self-employed. In so doing, more of your expenses may be deductible, but in exchange for that one benefit you lose the ability to claim unemployment and are on the hook for 100% of your Social Security taxes. Working in foreign countries complicates this even further, requiring you to stay on top of totalization agreements to make sure you aren't overtaxed on your overseas income. At present, we have no mechanism whereby it would be possible to acquire health insurance as a benefit of short-term employment with our multiple employers, and no available pension plan, putting the burden of saving for retirement almost entirely on you. All of this, combined with the difficult truth that every employer will pay you as little as they possibly can get away with, paints a pretty bleak picture. It's no wonder opera singers have a reputation for being hypercompetitive and undercutting of their colleagues. It's easy to feel like the only way to get ahead is by trampling on the backs of your peers.
>
> This is the world bequeathed to you by your predecessors. Now for the hardest truth of all: we need you to save us. Your generation is the generation that will have the greatest impact on the future of our art form, and thus the future of our profession. All of that power, and all of that responsibility, rests with you. We need more than your voice, and your singular take on the roles you inhabit: we need your advocacy.
>
> As of this writing, there are multiple bills languishing in Congress that would resolve the tax difficulties we are facing at

present, most notably the Tax Fairness for Workers Act and the Performing Artist Tax Parity Act (PATPA for short). As of this writing, the National Endowment for the Arts is under relentless attack. We need our priorities to be addressed by our government, and the only way that will happen is if you take an active interest in politics. All art is political— we sit on the sidelines at our peril.

You also must recognize that there is power in numbers, and we are much stronger as a community of artists in pursuit of the same goals than we could ever be fighting our own battles a contract at a time. Entertainers and artists of all stripes are ripe for exploitation because we love what we do so much; the temptation to work for less than we are worth is overwhelming. This is why the labor movement is essential to our survival. When we insist on bargaining collectively with our employers, the outcome is always better than going it alone. The American Guild of Musical Artists (AGMA) is our union, and it was founded to unite us all to achieve fair working conditions and equitable compensation, but unions don't function without the active participation of their members. They thrive only when their members stand together to fight for the collective good with determination and focus. We need your voice in every conceivable sense. Use it in the practice room, use it on stage, use it at the ballot box, and join your voice with those of your colleagues to fight for a stronger union. The way things are is not the way things have to be. It's on your generation to save us all, and I believe you can, and you will.

Summary of Key Principles

1 *As a singer, you are a small business owner.* That has consequences for your finances and taxes, among other things.
2 *Budgeting is an easy way to give yourself peace of mind and feel like you make more than you do.* When you know where your money is coming from and going ahead of time, there is significantly less anxiety in your day-to-day life. This is especially important for freelancers with irregular incomes.
3 *Consider getting a side job between (or even on) jobs to keep your finances stable.* Most companies you will work for early on will not pay per diem, so you will live out of pocket for the entire three-to-five-week contract.
4 *Be sure to plan for the future.* There may come a day when the phone stops ringing with singing opportunities, and you will need a plan for supporting yourself through your post-career years.

Find a financial advisor and find out how you can start saving on your current income.

5 *Take pride in your craft and stand up for yourself.* No one is as interested in your survival and growth as you are. Get involved in your union, pay attention to the working conditions around you and speak up when they are unacceptable. Speak up for singers who have less sway than you do—both at companies and in collective bargaining negotiations. Somewhere along the line, someone spoke up so your working conditions could be better.

Application Questions

1 Do I have external financial support to help me through the early stages of my career?
2 Do I have marketable skills that can help me earn the money I will need to fund audition tours, lessons, continuing education, and Pay-to-Sings?
3 Which of my expenses count as tax write-offs?
4 What are my options for retirement savings?
5 How do I create a written monthly budget to help me control my income in terms of my future plans?
6 How do I find a tax preparer and financial planner to help me manage my money? What are some questions I could ask them in order to determine whether they are well-suited for helping itinerant artists?

Bookmarks

- GSA Per Diem/MIE Rates (www.gsa.gov/travel/plan-book/per-diem-rates)
- Dave Ramsey's Budgeting Tools (www.daveramsey.com/tools)—Budgeting tools (including an app and paper forms) to help you get started with your personal budgets.
- LegalZoom's Guide to Choosing a Business Structure (www.legalzoom.com/business/business-formation/compare.html)—This page lays out some of the basic structural differences among the various structures mentioned in this chapter.
- Jeremiah Johnson's Financial Planning for Artists (www.TheMoneyMusician.com)
- QuickBooks Self-Employed (www.quickbooks.intuit.com/self-employed/)
- Expensify (www.Expensify.com)—Receipt capture app
- Shoeboxed (www.Shoeboxed.com)—Receipt capture app

- Springboard Exchange (www.springboardexchange.org)—Platform created by Minnesota-based Springboard for the Arts for artists to share and be inspired by stories of artists impacting communities, as well as resources and toolkits to help artists build their own impactful projects.
- "Work of Art" Toolkit Workbook (www.springboardforthearts. formstack.com/forms/woatoolkitrequest)—Enter your contact information to request this amazing *free* workbook that helps guide you through various stages of creative business development.

Build Your Business

1. Write a budget for next month. Look at your bank and credit card statements and figure out what you realistically spend each month in every category. If some of these numbers shock you, reduce your budget, and take the allotted amount out in cash at the beginning of the month.
2. Make a list of jobs you could do to keep yourself afloat while you get your career off the ground. Are there options that offer a high rate of pay and flexibility? Focus your attention here. Are you *good* at something, but not yet hirable? Look for training opportunities, including LinkedIn Learning (formerly Lynda) and local classes, which could get you up to a professional level for a reasonable investment. Any time-consuming or creative task that you have done to advance your career is potentially something you could to for another artist for a reasonable fee.
3. Decide on a system for tracking your job-related expenses and start tracking them *today*.
4. Do some research to determine whether there is a tax preparer in your area or who is trusted by your network who has expertise in the world of performing artists' taxes. Set up a consultation (and pay if you need to—it's worth it!) and begin to get some answers about your best approach to your business and tax preparation going forward.

Notes

1 Company-booked travel is fairly easy to get with most companies that have a full-time artistic administrator. In most cases they will book your travel using your loyalty accounts and Known Traveler Number. If not, it is easy to call the airline and add them on after the fact. (Can't miss out on Pre-Check!) If the company does not have the infrastructure in place to book your travel for you, you must insist on getting your reimbursement upon

arrival. By paying for your own travel, you are extending an interest-free loan to the company for a matter of weeks or months—a position in which singers should not be placed but are, with increasing regularity.
2 If you are able to negotiate a per diem (and the company codes it as such—double check your 1099/W2 to be sure), this money is not reported as income, but replaces the GSA Per Diem Rate you might otherwise file. If your manager negotiates a per diem for you, try to ask for it to be set aside as such in the contract; managers should not take commission on per diem (these are living expenses, not compensation), but if it is rolled into your total fee, they may.
3 I suspect this will be difficult to secure, especially without an agent working on your behalf, as it is not commonplace, and some smaller companies may not have the cash flow to provide this. Among other protections enjoyed by union artists, AGMA signatories are required to place an amount equal to every performer's fee in escrow at the beginning of the rehearsal period so the singers are guaranteed to be paid; there is no such guarantee of cash on hand with non-union houses.
4 With the exception of those included in the GSA "Per Diem" covered above, I am unaware of any allowance for any of these expenses, so you *must* keep receipts with notes to explain their applicability to your career, in case you are audited. By contrast, all you need to track in order to claim the per diem allowance is the number of days you were in each city, plus travel days to/from each city.
5 No advice given here by the author or other contributors in this chapter should be construed as coming from a tax or personal finance professional. As always, if you have specific questions regarding your business' income, expenses, or other areas that have tax-related consequences, you should seek the advice of a qualified tax professional.
6 In the current (2020) United States tax environment (the 2017 "Tax Cuts and Jobs Act," or "TCJA"):

- work-related deductions are limited to 1099 income; and
- the standard deduction is roughly $12,000 for a single filer and $24,000 for joint filers.

From a tax preparation standpoint, this means that most singers are likely to benefit from taking the standard deduction for the time being.
7 Note that the GSA gives a reduced MIE Rate for travel days, and that rate is supplied in the chart on the given website.

Reference

Jeremiah Johnson, phone conversation with the author, October 8, 2019.

11 Auditions, Rep Books, and Pianists

Short of political office and the NFL Combine, auditions in opera are potentially the most difficult and expensive job interview in the world. With so much committed in terms of financial, physical, and emotional resources, it feels as though there is a tremendous amount riding on a singer's brief five to ten minutes in the audition room. With so much that the singer can't control, we need to take advantage of everything we *can* control. This chapter will address the fundamental questions a singer encounters in the run-up to audition season (finding auditions, finding pianists, preparing repertoire) along with some tips for improving your auditions once the season is underway.

Finding and Applying for Auditions

The audition "season" for young singers begins each year around July 1—it is around this time that the first YAPs post their applications, with the first due dates around mid- to late August for auditions throughout the autumn. Almost all YAP and PTS auditions are now posted on YAP Tracker and many are also on Auditions Plus, and most require some mix of the following materials:

- résumé
- head shot
- application fee (these average around $35–40 and obviously add up quickly)
- references (typically 2–3)
- recordings (video and/or audio, usually must be no more than two years old).

Look at your YAP and Company databases and determine which opportunities to target in this round of applications. If you use my

YAP List, you'll find that I also make a note of when each YAP typically posts, so you won't miss it and won't have to check every day, either.

If you need references, reach out to them *before* you enter them into the YAP Tracker application, as in most cases, YAP Tracker immediately emails links to the references you enter.

Save Time and Money

It is helpful in the midst of applying for a dozen or more programs to try to cluster auditions whenever you can to take advantage of economies of scale. If you have a choice of dates and cities, try to cluster your first and second choices among many programs on the same days in the same cities.[1] Audition travel is expensive, and if you can knock out three auditions for the price of one plane ticket and one or two nights in an Airbnb or on a friend's couch, you should do it. Also, if you cluster them, try to book a single pianist who will play all of them for you—that way you have a single point of contact for your music and you get increasingly more comfortable with each audition. If you are in school, this approach has the potential benefit of only having to ask for a few days in a row off during a production, rather than asking the director to work around three to four trips for you (and presumably others in the cast).

Audition Repertoire

Audition repertoire strategies change as you move from YAPs to main stage work. While YAPs tend to favor a generalist approach, typically requiring four to five arias—including one in each of three to four languages, a Mozart or Handel, and a piece from the "long 20th century"[2]—by the time you are auditioning for main stage work, you should begin to have a sense of what repertoire shows you off the best, and include only that. If you are a tenor whose voice loves Rossini, you may not find any use in offering German or Russian Romantic music—that is up to you and completely valid in this context. In main stage auditions, you are no longer "checking boxes," but highlighting your strengths as an artist as they correspond to a company's needs.[3] In any case, your audition binder should have at minimum these five arias plus one or two "preview" or "stretch" arias (arias that indicate where you think your voice may go in the next three to five years) and a Golden Age musical theater piece or two.

> ### The Annual YAP Tracker Purge
>
> Just before the start of every application season, you should go through YAP Tracker (as well as any other place that saves your materials for you) and refresh your materials—delete old iterations and replace them with new ones.
>
> For reference, shelf life on your materials is as follows:
>
> - résumé: six months, maximum,
> - headshot: as long as it looks like you, or around five years at maximum,
> - recordings: generally two years, though some applications give only a 12-month window,
> - biography: 6–12 months, depending on how much activity you've had.
>
> My second summer at Utah Festival Opera, I had talked with enough people about résumé and application questions that we decided to do a "YAP Tracker Party"—we chose one afternoon where we all gathered in one apartment with our laptops and updated our materials: our résumés, bios, headshots, recordings, and websites. If people had formatting questions about résumés, I offered help, but for the most part, it was about accountability for all of us—after working and singing all summer, we had new materials, we were all applying for programs, and we all had piles of old materials crowding our YAP Tracker accounts, so we picked a day and cleaned out the old and uploaded the new, and started sending out applications right there. It was a great afternoon that I hope other Young Artists in other programs will adopt, because updating those materials is an easy thing to put off until the last minute. With our friends around, it was just a fun way to pass an afternoon.

What to Bring

Once you have booked your audition and travel, your attention should turn to what you must have with you in the audition. Some companies print your materials and have them on hand, but it is still a good idea to bring two to three copies of each of the following:

1 résumé
2 headshot
3 repertoire sheet

or:

1   press kit
2   repertoire sheet

plus one extra repertoire sheet for the accompanist to help them find your arias when they are called.

Repertoire Sheets/Aria Lists

Since we are concerned with professionalism in everything, we should not neglect our repertoire sheets in our visual branding, so use the same font scheme as your résumé.
 The essential information to include is:

- name
- voice type
- email/phone number.

and for each aria:

- title
- opera
- composer (last name is fine).

If you are performing a particularly long aria with several distinct sections, it is helpful to give each section as a potential starting/ending place (many administrators know them anyway and will ask specifically). For example, Zerbinetta's aria from *Ariadne auf Naxos* may be offered as follows:

"Großmächtige Prinzessin" (or Zerbinetta's Aria[4])

Ariadne auf Naxos
Strauss

1   "Großmächtige Prinzessin ..."
2   "Noch glaub'ich ..."
3   "So war es mit Pagliazzo ..."
4   "Als ein Gott ..."

The Repertoire Book

Throughout this book, in any matter addressing an outward-facing part of your presentation, I have advocated one guiding principle above all: appearing professional at every stage of your career. Others have put it in different terms: dress for the job you want. This should apply to everything that someone sees when they see you, from clothes to bag to shoes to résumé and head shot to … yes, your repertoire book.

Now, take a step back and look at your repertoire book or binder objectively. Keeping in mind that pianists often have relationships unknown to you with presenting organizations, what does this book say about you to an accompanist? How easy is it to navigate as someone who doesn't know their way around your book? If the audition panel says, "we'd like to hear the Verdi," how quickly could a pianist who didn't know your book find their way to that piece? Are your tempi, cuts, and ornaments clearly notated? Does the page have unnecessary clutter[5] or a missing bass staff at the bottom? Does the tab take the accompanist to the recitative when you're starting at the aria proper?

An accompanist can be a huge source of either confidence or anxiety for you, and this is largely in your control—the information you give them in your book and the few seconds of interaction you have before you start singing will determine to a great extent how your audition goes. As the old software and data management maxim goes, "Garbage In, Garbage Out." So let's begin by cleaning up any "garbage" that's interfering with our collaboration with the pianist.

Clean Copies and Clear Markings

There are at least two inviolable rules for repertoire books: (1) Clean copies and (2) Clear markings. If a mark isn't going to help a pianist play your piece, it should not appear in your repertoire book. I recommend having two separate copies of your book—one for the pianist, and one for the singer[6]—in order to keep markings in each relevant to the end user. (It is a good idea to bring your book to an experienced pianist for final approval.)

Your music copies should be:

- Double-sided;
- Placed directly in the book/binder with NO sheet protectors (you can never predict the lighting in an audition room, and sheet protectors can create glare that makes your music hard to read);
- Dark enough to read every note, dynamic, and tempo marking;
- Light enough that extra marks from the copier don't interfere.

Helpful markings include:

- Cuts (to the best of your ability, eliminate the music being cut by copying with a blank sheet of paper over excluded music);
- Starting/ending points (see above: if there are multiple starting points offered—i.e. recitative, cantabile, cabaletta—include marks and/or tabs for each);
- D.S/D.C./Coda marks highlighted (better yet, add the D.C. or D.S. material as extra pages—with unnecessary music eliminated—to save the pianist from having to flip and find it on the fly);
- Cadenzas written in, at least partially, so the pianist knows when to rejoin you;
- Tempo variations (stretches, etc.);
- Breath marks and fermatas that are not already part of the score (feel free to highlight them even if they are, especially if it's important that you have some room to take a breath in a particular spot).

The Book

I am not a fan of binders as rep books. I know they are easy, and most students have a dozen empty ones sitting around waiting to be used. But in most cases, they are also oversized (most common seems to be the 1" binder holding about 20 pages of music, which is thick enough to make traveling with two identical copies of your binder cumbersome), and pages seem to rip more easily in them than in other formats.

My personal recommendation is to get your repertoire book printed at a print shop every season. The final product will be well under ½" thick, which will make traveling with two copies easy. I use their black or blue vinyl cover for both front and back, and a comb binding (so arias may be swapped in and out as the season progresses).[7] You may prefer a spiral binding, which has the benefit of being more durable than the comb binding, but which—according to one coach I talked to—tends to sag against the piano, making page more turns difficult. I know coaches who prefer both, so check with yours.

Organizing the Book

Use whatever organization scheme you find most logical; I divide mine into two sections, "Arias" and "Party Tunes," the latter of which includes Golden Age musical theater and Great American Songbook favorites that I offer at auditions and donor events. It is good to have one or two of these available at every audition, just in case.

Here are two possible ways to organize and tab your book:

Method #1: Numbered Tabs

1. Create a Table of Contents with Aria Name, Opera Name, and Tab #
2. Affix tabs[8] to the back of the page before page 1 of each aria[9]
3. Number each tab according to the Table of Contents.

Method #2: Written Tabs

1. Affix large, sturdy plastic tabs to the back of the page before page one of each aria
2. *Clearly* mark each aria with title and/or composer.

(Tip: if tabs are numbered with marker, place a small piece of clear tape over them to keep them from smudging as multiple thumbs and fingers flip through your book each season.)

Provide the pianist at each audition with the same repertoire list that you provide the audition panel. If you use numbered tabs, make sure you have written (in large print) the corresponding tab number next to each aria on your list so your accompanist may quickly locate the pieces called by you or the panel. (Your accompanist is your partner in appearing professional—give them every tool you can. A clean, easily navigable book is an easy way to do this.)

Caveat Cantor: Let the Singer Beware

There is always the possibility that a company will ask the accompanist what else is in the book (yes, and bypass the singer entirely), and it can look bad for the singer if the panel gets excited about a title they aren't prepared to offer. There are a handful of companies that have a reputation for engaging in these practices, and it is a great opportunity for a singer to look expertly prepared but is also a little risky. For singers just starting out, I highly recommend only traveling with arias that you are ready to perform, just in case. Keep the arias you are working on with your teacher in a separate book (the "singer" copy of your repertoire book is a good place).

Always Have Backup

Cloud storage products[10] allow you to keep copies of your documents online, accessible from anywhere. It is good (and easy) practice to keep entire copies of your repertoire book and all of your audition materials backed up to a cloud storage account for easy access, just in case. You never know if you might forget your book in your hotel or drop it in a slushy puddle on a New York street in December. You will be relieved beyond words when the solution to your problem is as close as the nearest FedEx or Staples.

Pianists

Once you have auditions lined up and your repertoire book in order, it is time to address the matter of your audition pianist. The audition pianist has the potential to be either a great comfort or a source of anxiety for the singer, so singers should take every precaution to ensure a smooth audition—especially if the pianist is unknown to the singer or provided by the company.

Finding a Pianist

Many auditions provide a pianist (some for an additional fee, some for no fee), and most reputable houses and programs use reputable pianists that you can rely upon with confidence. Perhaps you have an audition that requires you to bring a pianist—or maybe you are offering non-standard repertoire that would benefit from a little more advance notice to the accompanist—and if you are traveling to the audition, you may have questions as to how to find a reliable one. Here are a few strategies I have used successfully:

1. For auditions outside of New York City, the first place you may want to look is at the university or conservatory featuring reputable voice programs. Start with coaching faculty and keep their information in your contacts. If they are unavailable for your audition, ask if they have a student or another area pianist they recommend.
2. In any city, you should of course feel free to ask not only your friends and colleagues in the area, but search and ask (search first) in online singer forums[11] for pianists recommended by other professional singers.
3. Don't forget to ask among your graduate school network—perhaps there are coaching alumni who have relocated to some of the cities you're auditioning in.

It is a good idea to do most of this legwork well in advance, if possible, so that you have plenty of options when the time comes.[12]

Auditions, Rep Books, and Pianists   123

> **Tip: Organizing Pianist Information in Your Contacts**
>
> Once you have pianists' contact information, you should make it as easy to find as possible. Here is what I recommend:
>
> 1 Put every pianist and all contact information in your phone
> 2 In the "Company" field, write "Pianist—[City]."
>
> If you find yourself needing a pianist, you can now search your phone contacts for "Pianist" and all of these will come up. Add "[City]" to your search if you want to narrow the list to a specific city.

Be on Your Best Behavior

Before you walk through the door into the audition it bears mention that while a singer is in public and in the vicinity of the audition venue, they are on display. This is especially true once the singer is inside the audition venue. Until you have been in the business for several years, you cannot possibly know everyone affiliated with every company you may be singing for. As such, it is best to comport yourself professionally as soon as you walk into the building where you are auditioning. A few things to be aware of:

1 Audition monitors have constant interaction with the audition panels. Treat them with the utmost respect. You can never know how close their relationship is to the company, but it is good to imagine that they have the panel's ear, just in case.
2 Try to be aware of other people around you. Audition venues (especially in New York) are cramped with singers, agents, pianists, administrators, heavy coats, suitcases, and palpable anxiety. Especially if you are calm and comfortable in these situations, try to give others space to go through their processes without loud or persistent distractions.[13]
3 Be ready to go early, if possible. No one will force you to go early but know that companies are as likely to run ahead as to run late and being prepared and unflappable sends a good message about your professionalism.
4 DO NOT WARM UP IN THE BATHROOM. Many of the more popular audition venues have additional studios for rent by the hour or fraction of an hour. I personally rent one at almost every

audition to help me shift my focus away from the hubbub of the city and into auditions, to change, and to warm up. The cost is usually very reasonable (often $8–15) and the benefit to your singing and mindset can be substantial.

Setting the Stage

You were granted an audition, so you coached your arias, booked a flight and a place to stay, booked a pianist, printed all of your materials in triplicate, flew to New York or Chicago or San Francisco, and the day has finally arrived: ten hours of round-trip travel for about ten minutes of face time to try to book this gig. It is hard not to get nervous, to let the moment grow 12 heads, to let your breath get short and your heart speed up. But these totally natural factors need to be harnessed into your most focused, most proficient ten-minute performance. No problem, right?

Calming oneself in the face of all the emotions that accompany an audition tour requires either ice water in one's veins or a regimen of preparation and visualization leading up to the audition to take yet more of the unknowns out of the equation.[14]

Here are some things you can do to turn some of the unknowns into knowns before your audition:

- Find out (via email or phone call, or at the last moment, the audition monitor) who will be in the room for your audition. Look them up (as you likely already did in Chapter 7). Know as much as you can about their preferences. Get their faces in your head. Picture them sitting at the table watching you sing.
- Find out what room the audition will be in. Whether it is one of the big audition venues in New York or a room at the company's facility, see if there is a photograph of that room on the website. Picture where the piano will be, how far away the panel will be. Try, if you can imagine such things, to imagine the acoustic in that room, how it will carry or dampen your voice. How many steps will you take from the door to the piano? Where will you put your bag? Your water?
- Determine how you will introduce yourself and your first selection. Imagine they prompt you in two or three different ways ("What would you like to sing for us?" "What would you like to start with?" "And who are you?") and think about whether your phrasing needs to change. Will you speak first to the accompanist or the panel?

- Work out what you will say to the pianist. Use the actual copy of your repertoire book that you will use in the audition. Rehearse it with your coach. Memorize how you will quickly and clearly convey all of the information you need for your collaboration to be successful.

This may all seem excessive, but it is based on the principle introduced at the beginning of this chapter: with so many things we cannot control in an audition setting, we must prepare those things we can. All this preparation helps us channel our anxiety productively and perform our best possible audition.

Showtime

The monitor calls your name. They either ask for your documents so they can convey them to the panel or they open the door for you, at which point you will deliver the documents yourself. (Follow the panel's lead regarding chit-chat; *do not* try to force it upon them.)
 Greet anyone who greets you, then go directly to the pianist. Hand them your book, open to the aria you will sing first, and place the repertoire sheet next to or behind your book on the piano; point out what it is and how to use it.
 Give the beginning tempo for your aria quietly and confidently (sing it in your head first so you know it is right), and briefly communicate any changes to the standard layout of the piece. Give additional tempi for the cabaletta or other sections, point out D.C./D.S. roadmap issues and any cuts. All of this should take about 15 to 20 seconds, max. Remember: the panel is waiting.
 Once you have communicated this information clearly, turn and face the audition panel, and interact with them. Let them prompt you to begin.[15]
 If the panel asks for subsequent arias, repeat this process; excuse yourself for a few seconds to establish your tempi, and point out the potential problem spots before turning back to the panel and beginning the aria.

I Just ... Oop (Getting Out of Sync)

No matter how professional you and your accompanist are, you can't control for everything. Occasionally, you will get out of sync. Remember, though, that every instance of adversity under pressure is an opportunity to demonstrate professionalism, poise, and polish. If you and your pianist get out of sync for whatever reason, remain calm and *control the moment*.

Here are a couple of optional scripts for interacting with the panel in such a moment:

- "I'm sorry,[16] that was not very good. Do you mind if I try it again?"
  If you do it with confidence and stay lighthearted (i.e. do not spiral)—and then actually execute the passage correctly—this can be an effective way to signal self-awareness and professionalism. (Do not do this twice in the same audition.)
- "I'm sorry. We are out of sync. Do you mind if we try that again?"
  It can be tricky to recover from a situation in which the pianist is not following your tempo, or where you didn't give the correct tempo. Without throwing the pianist under the bus—a classic nervous amateur mistake—acknowledge that the tempo is wrong, and you need a moment with your collaborator to get back in accord.
- Do nothing. Find your way back.
  This is only problematic if you and your pianist are actively trying to follow each other back to the same place, chasing a moving target.

Mistakes happen to everyone. Again, the most important thing is to appear professional, and in control without being self-deprecating or groveling.

The Waiting is the Hardest Part

After you leave your entire heart and soul on the floor of the audition room, pack your things, and head home, you will wait—sometimes days, sometimes months, and sometimes interminably. In time, you may receive an offer, or be wait listed, or receive the dreaded "PFO."[17]

If you have not received a response to your audition within a reasonable time, it is acceptable to reach out to the company to see when they may be making offers and notifying others.[18]

If you have been wait-listed and received other offers, it is acceptable to reach out to the company at which you're wait-listed and let them know you remain "enthusiastic about the possibility of singing with them," but that you have "received other offers and would like to get back to them" in short order. Don't be pushy, but don't get pushed around.

> ### Tip: Preparing for Everything
>
> It may help you to work in your lessons on various approaches to recovering in trouble spots. Find the places most likely to present a pitfall for you or an unfamiliar pianist and rehearse your response to each.

Dealing with Rejection

Opera singers (and actors and dancers) are warriors—the amount of rejection inherent to our work is staggering, and I think it's important that we honor that in ourselves and our colleagues. So when we *don't* get a gig, what can we do? First and foremost, I think it is important to acknowledge how crummy it is to not get a gig, and that the feelings associated with that are legitimate and the disappointment is real and consequential. Be gentle with yourself.

So when I don't get a gig that I really hoped for, I gauge my feelings about it, and allow myself up to 48 hours to grieve in whatever way I decide to. Essentially, this is 48 hours where I'm not allowed to pick apart my recordings, my performance, look up who got it, or plan any corrective action in myself. I let it sit, allow the most intense disappointment to pass, and then I get to work. If I have a recording of the audition, I might take it to my teacher. If the auditors offer feedback (they almost never do, except through your agent), I bring that to my teacher, as well.

But here is the deal I have made with myself as part of this career: I must always be getting better. Maybe it's a new aria, maybe it's polishing an old aria I take for granted, maybe it's working on languages or character development, maybe I decide to do another layer of preparation for the next audition that I didn't do for this one. Once the grieving period is over, it's time to make a plan and get better. And some days, you're going to sing your best and just plain get out-sung. That is the mathematical reality of this career, and it's out of your control, so you can't spend time worrying about that. Control the things you can and give yourself over to the complete randomness of what you can't.

Summary of Key Principles

1 *Auditions are stressful, but necessary,* so learn to control every aspect that it is in your power to control.

2   *Auditions are expensive*, so look for economies of scale in everything from travel to printing to accompanists.
3   *Pianists are your partner and lifeline in an audition*, so work to make everything in their world easier, from a clean repertoire book to clear instructions. And *never throw them under the bus.*
4   *Visualization is a very powerful tool for overcoming anxiety*, and thorough research can fuel effective visualization. Try to overcome fear of the unknown by moving more things into the "known" column.
5   *Perfect practice makes perfect.* Rehearse everything that you can in order to counteract any panic that may set in if things go awry during auditions. Rehearse starts and stops, scripts, spots where you might get out of sync with the pianist.
6   *Maintain professionalism before, during, and after the audition.*

Application Questions

1   Is my current repertoire binder/book easy to follow, and free of extraneous markings?
2   Is my binder/book easy to travel with? Can I easily pack two copies in a bag that is small enough to bring to an audition?
3   Is my repertoire backed up in its entirety online, so that it's easily accessible in an emergency?
4   What is the most important information I can communicate to the audition pianist about each of my audition pieces?
5   Do I know any pianists in New York, Chicago, or Philadelphia? What about other cities?

Bookmarks

- Classical Vocal Reprints (www.ClassicalVocalRep.com)—A vocal music store run by Glendower Jones, who has served the singing world with distinction for decades. If you can't find what you're looking for on his site, reach out via email or Facebook; it is rare that he doesn't have what we're looking for. Classical Vocal Rep and its proprietor are part of a dying breed of high-touch, high-information music sales that we can't afford to lose. Just about anyone you ask in the industry will tell you: this is where you should buy your scores.
- Winning on Stage (www.WinningonStage.com)—A site devoted to peak performance in performing artists, run by Dr. Don Greene, a long-time sports psychologist to the United States Olympic track and field teams.

Auditions, Rep Books, and Pianists 129

Build Your Business

1. Examine your repertoire binder/book and make sure it objectively meets high standards of cleanliness and legibility, and that all information that a pianist needs is clearly marked.
2. Back your entire audition book up to a cloud-based storage service.
3. Compile a list of pianists in major audition cities and input them into your phone so that they are easily searchable when you are panicked and rushed (i.e. searchable without remembering their names), in case of a last-minute cancellation or audition.
4. Run your arias in your lesson and determine:
   a. Potential pitfalls and how you'll recover from each;
   b. The most important information you need to communicate to a pianist. Figure out how to communicate this information in about 15 seconds per aria.

Notes

1. Unfortunately, companies seem to be less and less inclined to make audition season easy on singers, coming to New York and other cities at increasingly random times (like mid-September) for YAP auditions and then occasionally choosing to do main stage auditions before Thanksgiving, taking them outside of the annual pilgrimage dates between Thanksgiving and December 22nd or so.

   With YAPs, it is also becoming common to pair these early auditions with early offers and quick (read: one week) acceptance windows before a singer is replaced with the next on the list. Presumably it is to ensure that a program gets its choice of singers before those singers have other options, but it is a bit unfair in my opinion—considering all that a singer sacrifices to apply and travel to multiple auditions, to then have to accept an offer before knowing the full range of possibilities their efforts have earned them. But this is a business, and businesses by and large are primarily serving a constituency other than their labor pool.

2. In many cases, companies now specify post-1950 or even 21st-century arias. It is a good idea at this point to identify a 21st-century aria to keep in your package for these scenarios. Occasionally, companies will accept (or even specify) a Golden Age musical theater piece (pre-1960—think Rodgers & Hammerstein) in place of the contemporary aria.

3. There are still several companies who post main stage auditions without announcing specific repertoire. I think this is an artifact of the economic downturn in 2007/8 when seasons were reduced, and companies weren't as certain that they could pull off their top choice repertoire. Or perhaps they like to announce their repertoire later in the season and don't want it to leak to their audience. Either way, I find it a questionable practice,

both at the YAP and main stage level, especially since some companies are charging application fees to main stage singers now.
4   There are some famous arias for which it is perfectly acceptable to refer to them by something other than their title, especially when it is the character's only aria (e.g. "Zerbinetta's aria," "Gremin's aria"). Be careful and check with knowledgeable coaches or teachers before doing so. I suspect it would raise eyebrows to inform a panel that you were opening with "Pamina's aria" rather than simply, "Ach, ich fühl's." Again, it is always good practice to check with knowledgeable people rather than going rogue and risking looking amateurish. In this case, it is acceptable to list and refer to this aria as "Zerbinetta's Aria."
5   Unhelpful clutter includes translations, phrase markings for the singer, IPA, or any writing that serves non-musical purposes.
6   One alternative, of course, is having one clean copy of your binder with markings for the pianist and your copies all in PDF format on a tablet. You should use the format you prefer, of course. I like paper copies.
7   The binding and cover together cost about $5 on top of the printing. I tend to at least re-bind my book every year, in addition to replacing one or two arias. So the startup cost (printing and binding from scratch) might be $15–20, but refreshing it each year is more like $5–8. Not bad.
8   Use sturdy plastic or laminated cardstock tabs like ones made by Post-It. I do not recommend using paper or the flimsy plastic ones used to flag lines in contracts, et al. The thin ones crease, move, and tear, and look horrible. The sturdy plastic ones will last you multiple seasons.
9   If the syntax here is confusing, the reason for attaching to the back of the last page of the previous aria is so that when the tab is pulled, it (1) opens directly to the beginning of the aria in question, and (2) stays affixed because the pulling motion doesn't pull it away from the paper.
10 At the time of publication, the most ubiquitous ones are Google Drive, Dropbox, OneDrive, and Box, but there are certainly others. Most, if not all, of these can interface seamlessly with self-service printers at FedEx Office and Staples.
11 For example the "New NEW Forum for Classical Singers (NNFCS)," "Chicago Area Classical Singers Group," "Classical Singers of Color Resource & Support Group (CSCRSG)," "Philadelphia Area Classical Singers," and "Accompanist Connection (NYC)" on Facebook.
12 *N.B.* You may find yourself in a situation where your pianist cancels at the last possible moment, or you have a last-minute opportunity to audition but need to furnish your own pianist. It may be as easy as asking in the hallway at one of the big venues (Shetler, National Opera Center, etc.) during audition season, but on a day when there is less happening at a venue, having these pianists' contact info handy will be very helpful.
13 This includes having long, name-droppy conversations (we all have them, don't pretend) where you get to list every gig you've had in six months. Try to imagine that the people in earshot have never booked a gig and have spent money they don't have to be here in the hope of booking their

first. The empathy and emotional intelligence singers famously spend their lives developing will go a long way here. Just be aware.
14. See Don Greene's important and groundbreaking work on the psychology of peak performance and auditioning in musicians. In addition to several books (*Performance Success, Audition Success,* and *Fight Your Fear and Win*), he offers a variety of assessments and online courses at his website, www.WinningOnStage.com.
15. If you have a particular dramatic beat or action (e.g. "I lean on the piano with my back to the panel, then lift my head") after which you want the pianist to begin, let them know this, as well.
16. These are exceptions to my general rule of never saying you're sorry in rehearsal or audition situations—such an action very subtly changes the power dynamic and transmits that you do not consider yourself equal to the other professionals in the room. It's touchy, but I think the best action in almost every scenario is to acknowledge an error and fix it without apologizing. Apologies in those settings make everyone feel awkward.
17. A rejection email—a response so ubiquitous and so often poorly executed it has earned the nickname, "PFO," for "please (bugger) off."
18. YAP Tracker has a tracking mechanism built in that indicates when offers have been received, though it is, in most cases, reported by recipients, so it depends on successful candidates' promptness in noting the offer in their own profiles' tracking section.

12 Beyond #bookedandblessed
Working in an Opera House

You have completed the auditions, received the contract, and done your preparation, and now we get to the good stuff: new colleagues, enthralling productions, rehearsals, the orchestra, the audience, the glowing reviews ...

I don't want to get ahead of myself, but this is the part we work so hard for—this is the payoff. But showing up to work your first day at a YAP, a main stage gig, or even a Pay-to-Sing can be somewhat bewildering even as it exhilarates. This chapter breaks down what to expect on the "first day of school"[1] at the two main categories of opera gigs and attempts to help you navigate the unfamiliar terrain of your new life as a professional singer.

Day Zero

Once you have a gig on the books, your real work begins: preparing your musical assignments. This is Day Zero. As a professional main stage artist, thorough musical preparation is the bare minimum expectation. But your preparation can also distinguish you to the extent that you have internalized not just the notes, rhythms, and phrasing, but the character, the dramatic intention, and even some bold choices in the music or drama of your character.

Memorizing Music

Perhaps the most underappreciated aspect of their job is that opera singers must memorize staggering amounts of music on a continual basis. To some, memorizing music comes easily—the structure of it, the text, the rhythm and melody all stick without superhuman effort. To others, memorizing music is a Sisyphean grind. The memorization aspect of this career is one that will never change, so it is best to figure out your process before seeking paid work (including apprenticeships), so that you don't burn important bridges for lack of preparedness.

Prima le parole, dopo la musica!

In the opening scene of Strauss' Capriccio, Olivier and Flamand set up the fundamental question of the opera: Which is more important to opera, the words or the music? Olivier chooses the former, Flamand the latter. From an artistic standpoint, the question is perhaps a matter of taste, with passionate advocates in either camp; in terms of learning music, though, the consensus is clear: learn the words first, *then* the music. It makes sense when you think about it—in almost every opera, the drama of the character began in the text of the libretto and was realized in music by the composer afterward. The text is also, for most people, the hardest element to remember; melodies tend to stick in our minds more readily than prose.

David Holloway used to teach apprentice singers at Santa Fe Opera the "Rule of 25s"[2] that he utilized as a Fest baritone in Germany over many years:

- speak the text 25 times,[3] then
- speak the text in rhythm 25 times, then
- sing the line 25 times.

Experience confirms that having correctly performed these 75 recitations of each line or passage, the text is likely to be committed to memory, and the music of the line may well be, too. When I use this method, I write out my lines on a yellow legal pad with three checkboxes at the end of each line, as in Table 12.1:

Table 12.1 Tracking Holloway's "Rule of 25s," each "X" represents 25 perfect repetitions

Line	Text	Rhythm	Sung
Aprite un po' quegli occhi uomini incauti e sciocchi	X	X	
guardate queste femmine, guardate cosa son!	X		
Queste chiamate dee, dagli ingannati sensi	X		
a cui tributa incensi, la debole ragion!	X		

Preparing the Whole Artist

There are people in this business who will tell young singers—earnestly and with singers' best interests at heart—"if you can imagine doing anything else, do." With all due respect, I think this is horrible advice. Some of the most interesting artists I have ever met came from experiences and disciplines outside opera. Our personal interests and the way that we see the world make us whole humans, and that humanity helps us bring our characters to life. Why then would we see other interests or strengths as a sign that we don't belong? Sing opera as long as it is fun for you.

Day One: Training Programs

The first day of a training program typically features an orientation of sorts—the administration introduces itself to the singers, the singers introduce themselves to everyone, and before the day is over, you may all participate in a rite of passage called "Death by Aria" or the "Sing-In," in which every new apprentice/young artist sings their flashiest aria to assert their dominance.

The rest of your first day of a training program is likely to include a mix of rehearsals and individual coachings. In fact, for the most part, until tech week in your main stage productions, most days at a training program follow the same basic template: classes, coachings, lessons, and your rehearsals for main stage productions.

This is where you take your first "reps" as a professional singer: learning how to pace yourself, assimilate information on multiple musical pieces in the same day, build a character, and take care of yourself, and beginning to figure out who you are as a singer and an artist. It is not a bad idea to keep a journal documenting not only what you learn, but how your body and voice respond to different workloads, amounts of sleep and water, amounts of practice, warming up, and exercise—in some ways, you are conducting a laboratory experiment where you are both the observer and the subject. Take good notes and learn what you can about yourself.

Also, be aware that while you may be nervous and worry that everyone else in the program knows more than you do, the reality is that most of your peers are going through it for the first time, as well. *Trust your preparation* and enjoy the music-making. The stakes get a bit higher as you move into YAPs, but preparation and a healthy approach to growth and learning will serve you well at every level.

Day One: Main Stage

The first day of a professional main stage engagement is typically set aside for the full-cast sing-through—and is usually the only rehearsal the conductor gets for themselves until the *Sitzprobe*. At both of these rehearsals you will have your score out on a stand for reference, which is convenient for marking the conductor's preferences (this is the first time you will be learning how the conductor wants the score sung, so keep a pencil handy) and notes.

Always sing out in the sing-through. A singer should not mark[4] in the sing-through unless they are physically unable to sing. The first rehearsal is where the conductor and company management learn that everyone in the cast can sing their roles and is prepared to do so. Marking is for the third time through staging or running a scene in the same day.

It is also somewhat of a tradition that singers dress at least "business casual" for the sing-through, as it is the first impression and the singers will not be moving around learning staging. This is not a hard and fast rule, but this is another opportunity to err on the side of professionalism.

Rehearsal Types

In the course of rehearsing an opera, you may encounter most or all of the following rehearsals:

Sing-Through/Music Rehearsal—The first rehearsal of most production periods and one of two where your score will be handy.

Production/Concept Meeting—Some companies begin a production period by having the director (with or without the scenic and costume designers) explain the production concept to the cast. Here you might see costume sketches and computer renderings or models of the various sets.

Staging Rehearsal—The majority of rehearsals in a production period are devoted to working out staging. These rehearsals belong to the stage director, with the conductor and coach lending musical support. Sometimes the first rehearsal for a given scene will also feature a sing-through of the scene to be staged before moving on to blocking. These rehearsals can be very taxing on the voice, so listen to your body and feel free to mark after the first or second time through the scene at full voice.

Room Run/Designer Run—The last rehearsal before the production moves to the theater is a full show run with the lighting, projection, and sound designers in attendance.

Sitzprobe/Wandelprobe—Typically the first rehearsal of "tech week," the *Sitz* (sitting) or *Wandel* (changing/shifting) is also the first rehearsal with orchestra, and the last time with vocal scores. In a *Sitzprobe*, singers typically sit until their part, then stand to sing. In a *Wandelprobe*, singers are typically placed in the general area from which they sing a scene, but are not running staging; the emphasis in either case is on the singers and orchestra working together for the first time, and as such, this rehearsal belongs to the conductor.[5]

Technical ("Tech") Rehearsals—These rehearsals belong to the production crew, and they are meant to work out the timing of cues and scene changes as well as the technical aspects of any effects built into the show (lights, sound, drops, curtains, entrances, exits, plus fights and large crowd scenes). They may be accompanied by piano or orchestra (usually the former, because orchestras are expensive), but importantly, they are rarely costumed to any extent. The exception to that rule is if characters are wearing costume pieces that could provide difficulty in their interaction with the set. A common example might be having singers wear their costume shoes on a raked[6] stage or a set with stairs. These rehearsals can run very long, but often don't contain all music (especially arias), preferring to go "cue-to-cue" in order to get timing worked out.

Dress Rehearsals—These are the fully costumed runs that act as the final tune-ups and first performances in front of invited guests (including press). A typical production schedule might have a piano tech plus a piano dress and two orchestra dresses (the latter of which will have invited guests—usually donors) followed by a "dark" day with no run or performance before opening night.[7] Singers will often mark particularly difficult passages during this rehearsal, but this should be cleared with the conductor at least and perhaps the administration.

Stage Managers

Stage managers (collectively, SMs) are the behind-the-scenes conductors of all the show's technical aspects. If you have never worked with a stage manager before, or only worked with one in an academic setting, you will be duly amazed at the feats they perform in service to the show.

The Production Stage Manager (PSM) will run every rehearsal and is the person who "calls" the show once it moves to the theater. They are typically also the ones who will remind you to sign in at rehearsals and performances and will be the contact person for your complimentary tickets.

Assistant Stage Managers (ASMs) stand at entrance points backstage and their primary duties are to cue singer/actor entrances and scene changes for the crew in the wings.

Stage managers are miracle workers—overworked, over caffeinated, stressed-within-an-inch-of-their-lives miracle workers who arrive at the theater long before we do, stay long after, and get zero applause for their efforts. Their team is responsible for ensuring that every light cue, every singer entrance, every scene change, quick costume change, and sound effect in the show are perfectly placed. Treat them well, be where you're supposed to be on time, and when they ask you to be quiet, be quiet. If you notice in the course of rehearsals that any of the SMs have a go-to snack or drink, bring it to them on opening night with a short card expressing your appreciation for all they've done to put this show together. Seriously: you will never know how much you love stage managers until you do a show without them.

Traditions and Etiquette

Theater people generally and opera people specifically have some unwritten traditions and matters of etiquette that are worth knowing before you perform your first show. Here are a few to help you get started:

1 *"Toi, toi, toi"*[8]/*"In bocca al lupo"*[9]—"Good luck" greetings singers give each other and production crew before shows.
2 *Opening/Closing night gifts*—If you are a principal artist,[10] it is customary (but not mandatory) to give small gifts and/or cards to certain people in your productions to commemorate the show:
    a For the conductor, stage director, and your host (if you were housed with someone), a nice bottle of wine or box of chocolates is traditional;
    b For other principals, a small gift of food, liquor, wine, or a trinket of some sort is traditional;
    c For the chorus, a bag or two of candy (something that won't get on to their clothing or affect their singing is often the best option[11]) per dressing room;
    d Brief "thank you" notes are a nice touch for the people above, plus stage managers, your wig/makeup artist, your dresser, and the Artistic Administrator are a nice touch.
3 *Clapping on stage*—When the bows are staged at one of the tech or dress rehearsals, you may want to inquire about the house's preferences regarding clapping for your colleagues on stage and in the pit during the bows. It may come as a surprise, but some

companies have a strong preference against artists rendering applause from the stage, some prefer stomping (especially for acknowledging the orchestra), and some welcome artists' impulses to honor their colleagues with applause. It's a question worth checking in about before the final dress.

4 *Do not post audio or video from rehearsals online anywhere* without the specific permission of every person whose work is reflected on said recording. Audiences love behind-the-scenes footage, and as an artist, you should feel free to share moments from your private work sessions—but aside from the legal implications of broadcasting a performance of a union orchestra, for example, you and your colleagues have implicit rights to privacy, which includes controlling whether sounds you make in rehearsal are heard by anyone outside of that room.

Cover Etiquette

At some point in your career, you may find yourself "covering" (understudying) a role in a professional company. Cover assignments are incredible opportunities to learn a key role in your repertoire while you watch a world-class artist go through the process of putting it on stage. A few things to be aware of:

1 Be fully prepared as though you were singing the role from day one. If the principal artist has a travel delay or illness, you may be called upon to sing in the sing-through and early staging rehearsals.
2 Different artists treat their covers differently: some are collegial and generous, some ignore their covers, and some are inexplicably hostile. If you run into the latter, it is not your fault. And if you find yourself with a cover at some point, please treat them well.
3 Take detailed staging notes. Not only are you expected to know the staging and be ready to perform it at any time, but if the artist you are covering misses a direction in the course of a rehearsal, they will have both you and the stage manager available should they need you.
4 Be kind and collegial, and if you have the chance to ask questions of the principal artist, conductor, stage director, or stage manager, do.[12]

Other Responsibilities

As a principal artist, you may have other contractual obligations during the production period, and you may also have the chance to participate in other ways to help the company promote the show.

- *Donor functions*—Typically principal artists are expected to sing at a fundraising or appreciation dinner for the company's donors. Many of these people will be underwriting your performance fees, and these functions are a wonderful opportunity to give back in a personal way and to make a personal connection with the people who make our jobs possible.
- *Radio/TV promotion*—Occasionally a company has an opportunity to promote the production in local media outlets in the form of interviews with and broadcasted performances by the show's stars. These are not only great opportunities to help get the word out about the show, but very effective, free visibility boosters for the artists on social media.
- *Social media takeovers*—Many companies now engage their principal artists in "takeovers" of their social media accounts in the days leading up to the show. These are great opportunities to let the public see what "a day in the life" of an opera singer looks like, to promote the show and your own social media accounts. If you feel comfortable with the various platforms, you may find that this is a fun way to help the company promote your hard work.
- *Concerts*—You may also be asked to sing on one or more concerts during the production period. I find them to be a lot of fun, but they are also a potential area of abuse. My advice: be sure that the specifics of your participation are agreed upon and codified in your contract. Among the details you should not leave to chance: number of performances, corresponding excusal from rehearsals, repertoire (what/who provides/how early it is provided), transportation, dress code, and additional compensation.

Maintaining Relationships

Being on the road for weeks at a time takes a toll on relationships (not just romantic—think friends and family who rely on you or spend a lot of time with you when you are home—but for these purposes I am referring to romantic partnerships). Every relationship is different, but the common denominator to navigating the time apart successfully is communication. To give each party a chance to have their voices heard, I recommend you:

1 Talk to each other up front about expectations and needs.
2 Go over what daily schedules look like for each of you.
3 Find times during days (or at comfortable intervals) when your routines both allow time to speak (this can be hard to pin down if your schedule changes daily).

4   Continue talking about what is going well and what needs tweaking in order to meet each other's needs.
5   Do not hide your frustration, pain, or sadness from each other to "spare" the other.
6   Allow the routine to change according to each other's needs and try to be flexible with each other.[13]
7   Remember that you are going to experience the separation differently than them—you are in a new place with new people and engaging work to do; your partner is at home, going through your daily routine without their partner. So listen when they say they miss you and when they communicate a need.
8   Find ways to simulate your shared routine or make your partner's days easier from afar—send a rideshare to take them to work, send groceries, flowers, a cleaning service, dog walker, or gifts at random. Technology continues to find new ways to connect us, so listen closely to what is stressing them out and find creative ways to take some of the sting out of your absence.

All of us who work in the business know singers who maintain strong, happy family lives despite spending the better part of ten months on the road each year—and we know singers who have lost relationships and marriages to the various pressures that this career presents. One can no more guarantee their success than predict their failure in these things, but if there is anything of which I am certain, it is that open, stubbornly consistent communication is every relationship's best chance of survival.

It Takes a Village

The number of people involved in putting together a production as complex and expensive as an opera is many times the number we see on stage, and the typically short production period requires that everyone be fastidiously prepared and doing their job to a high degree of professionalism. At the same time, the theater is a warm place, marked by generous and wise colleagues, creativity, and vulnerability. It can be overwhelming to encounter the ever-larger companies as you climb the ladder in this business, but the rewards tend to increase in proportion to the responsibilities and scale. Be prepared and stay open, teachable, and grateful at every level and you will extract from this world many times what you put in.

Summary of Key Principles

1   *Being prepared is both the bare minimum and an easy way to distinguish yourself.* Commit yourself to being the most prepared

person in every cast—not just notes, rhythms, text, and style, but try to come to the table with thoroughly imagined characters and answers to your character's essential questions.

2   *Give yourself every chance to succeed.* You will work and sacrifice to unimaginable degrees in order to succeed in this career, so be honest with yourself about your desires and your limitations. If you have persistent difficulties with the foundational aspects of preparation/learning, consider seeking help from a counselor or doctor. It may not be your fault, but it *will* reflect poorly on you if you don't sort it out.

3   *Be considerate and appreciative of the skilled people around you,* from your cast mates to the music and production staff, to the chorus and orchestra, donors, and all of the people in the office who keep the lights on and bring audiences to see you. It is a near miracle every time an opera is produced. Most everyone around you is a skilled professional and contributes to the success of the production to an equal degree as you do.

Application Questions

1   What is my preparation process for roles and music? Are there weak spots in my process that could be strengthened by seeking help from colleagues, teachers, or others?
2   The next time you're in a production, try to notice: Who else is contributing to the success of this production, and in what way?
3   How can I pace myself—or give myself time to recover—during busy days in training programs?
4   If I have a romantic partner, what do they need from me while I travel? How can I take some of the sting out of my absence from time to time?

Bookmarks

- Lucia Lucas' website (www.0p3r4.com)

Notes

1   I know that some people find this phrase condescending and believe that it infantilizes the hard work, training, and artistry you have poured into your craft. I sympathize with this point and hope you don't feel condescended to—all I would say is that all of that is correct, and so you have earned the right to refer to your job in any way you see fit. If that is "first day of school" or some other thing, so be it. It's yours. You have earned it!

2 Lucia Lucas, a baritone who fested many years in Germany and who first learned this method from David Holloway at Santa Fe, has elaborated on this method and included her method of score preparation at her website, "0p3r4 (Opera) for Engineers."
3 It is crucial for this step that the 25 times are sequential and correct every time—it is worth restarting the entire process if you find you have worked an error into your recitation. We do not want the error to imprint in our memory.
4 "Marking" is singer-speak for not singing at full voice. There are two main marking strategies: singing quietly and singing down the octave. Many singers choose never to mark in rehearsal, preferring to acclimate their voices to the rigors of their roles along with the staging; others choose to mark strategically, allowing their voices time to rest and/or recover as needed. As you learn your voice and its limitations, you will develop your own best approach. Before a rehearsal or scene where you intend to mark, it is good practice to inform the conductor of your intention.

   I will say that I have been present in a sing-through where a conductor took a soprano repeatedly through several challenging scenes including a demanding aria and then subtly disparaged her by noting in front of the entire cast that a certain soprano he had worked with never omitted a certain optional high note in rehearsal. (No word, of course, on whether he ever subjected *her* to three or more passes through the long and demanding aria at the end of a sing-through of the role.) I want to be clear: that conductor's behavior was entirely unacceptable, and you as a singer are perfectly justified in marking after the first time through an aria or scene in a day. Do not let anyone bully you into doing damage to your voice—all anyone will remember later is that your voice was ragged for three days of rehearsal, not how it got that way. Protect your voice and your reputation at all costs.
5 Occasionally, a stage director (or very rarely, a choreographer) will try to intervene in a *Wandelprobe* if the staging wasn't quite right in the room run. If this happens, the conductor will usually intervene, but feel free to make a note of this to the stage manager, who can do so on the singers' behalf. This rehearsal is about music and *only* music. The singers and orchestra *must* be permitted to focus on getting in sync with each other. After all, the director has had weeks of staging time; the conductor gets the sing-through and the *Sitz/Wandel*, plus two to three orchestra read-throughs to get their part correct.
6 That is, slanted.
7 It is very rare, but occasionally companies have been known to sell tickets to a final dress rehearsal. If this is the case, I believe (as do most singers and agents, as far as I am aware) that the artists should be paid an additional performance fee unless an arrangement has otherwise been reached beforehand.
8 Pronounced, "toy, toy, toy" not "twah, twah, twah"—it is German (not French) and meant to mimic the sound of spitting over one's shoulder to fend off evil spirits.

9 Literally "into the mouth of the wolf," it is a traditional good luck wish in Italian theater. The traditional answer from the artist is, "crepi il lupo" ("may the wolf die").
10 If giving gifts would present a hardship for any reason, do not feel pressured to purchase them; a heartfelt note on a store-bought card is perfectly acceptable.
11 Swedish Fish, Starburst, Twizzlers, Haribo gummy bears, and Sour Patch Kids are favorites in the houses I have worked.
12 Again, artists are all different, but it is probably a good idea to keep your eagerness in check—let it drive your preparation and attentiveness, but don't be too quick to offer "help" to the principal artists. It is bad (the worst, really) form to give "notes" to your colleagues, and the principal artists you cover are your colleagues, so be careful not to say anything that could be construed as giving instruction, advice, or correction. That is not your role as a cover, and it can put even the most collegial singer on edge.
13 On my first gig, my wife and I Skyped every day, and she came to visit twice in eight weeks. A couple of years later, on a 13-week contract, we decided to text every day, talk every couple of days, and set up a standing Skype date on Sunday (my day off), and she visited twice. By the time I did that 13-week contract the second time, we had figured out that we could go about six weeks before we needed a visit to avoid falling out of sync and maintained the Sunday Skype date from the previous year. It's always a work in progress, but again—communicate and make adjustments!

Epilogue: The Best of All Possible Careers

For all its challenges, stresses, potential disappointments, and long hours, I really believe that singing the operatic art form may be the best of all possible jobs. But the odds are long—and as long as they are for certain voice types (hi, sopranos!), they are even longer for singers of color and people with disabilities. And of course, the more of those categories you personally fall into, the bleaker your outlook becomes. We have, alas, a very long way to go to before we can claim that opera is "for everyone."

As I have tried to convey several times throughout the course of this book, there is much about having a career in this business that is out of your hands—so you have to be diligent in those areas that you can. This much I can say for certain: *the opera world tends to make room for singers with a thoroughly realized and compelling personal artistry.* This is one of the most encouraging things I can say about the challenges we face as singers and is unfortunately one of the ways in which our existing education system is poorly equipped to prepare us. Voice programs in higher education tend to concern themselves primarily with technical proficiency—perhaps because it can be quantified and graded, unlike creativity and artistry. So until the American education system commits the required resources to the nurturing and development of creativity and artistry at every level, this aspect of who you are is primarily your responsibility: to seek inspiration, to examine and question all of the "way(s) it's done" and discard those that don't resonate or serve, and then to bring your boldest vision to the world's great stages—or to create another vehicle for delivering your art on your terms.

If that seems a tall order, I empathize, really. But the last thing opera needs right now is another technically-proficient-but-completely-generic "Una voce poco fa" or "Largo al factotum." If we care enough about opera to endure the poor pay and everything else, if we want to make the case for it to Generations X, Y, and Z, we have to learn to break their hearts, make them laugh, and make them examine their beliefs about all of the questions that our art form raises. And we have to be able to do it without leaning on a multi-million-dollar production budget for the fireworks. The essential material is already in place in each libretto and score.

I realize that this final chapter is of a different character than what has preceded it. I have used all of this ink to teach you how to navigate the business of singing as a professional: how to find the doors, what to bring when you knock on them, even what's waiting on the other side of them. But no amount of planning can replace your being the kind of artist that makes companies dream of excuses to hire you or inspires their patrons to call asking about you. That's up to you. Your professional "calling card" consists of a few simple, powerful data points:

1   your artistry
2   your reliability
3   your personality/collegiality.

Every one of those is in *your* control. If any of them are out of alignment, your career will suffer, and you with it. Develop and guard these three things jealously; you have worked too hard, dreamt too vividly, and sacrificed too much to miss out for reasons within your control.

If you aren't sure how to develop your personal artistry, I suggest you spend time watching great artists in every discipline. Look within it, too, but go as far outside of opera as you can to find inspiration (it is everywhere) and then sit with your thoughts about their ideas, performances, personal style, creativity.

See if something in them resonates in you. See if you can put that something into words, make it your own, or build on it.

Perfection isn't the point—art is. Art is perhaps the most powerful means our species has of communicating ideas and subverting biases. So, the world—and certainly the opera world—needs great, brave artists to tell the truth on stage and everywhere we go. The good news is that that bravery is part of our DNA: it is the same part that enables us to go to audition after audition, booking a job once out of every 10, 15, or 20 times; to listen to recordings of ourselves and diligently examine and address our technical shortcomings; to ask for the help we need to close the gap between where we are and where we want to be. Our art form is audacious and sublime and (though I know not everyone agrees) vital, and it requires unique artists to tell its stories—artists like you—to this generation and the next. If you want this "best of all possible jobs," I wish you every success and a good bit of luck along the way.

Glossary

agent A person who represents a group ("roster") of artists to presenting organizations and provides contract negotiation services.

American Guild of Musical Artists (AGMA) The labor union that represents the interests of opera and choral singers in addition to stage directors, and ballet dancers.

aria package The standard list of arias you bring to auditions. Also known as "your five."

Artist Diploma (AD) A graduate-level diploma awarded by some schools of music. Not an academic degree, but a common post-graduate step for younger graduates of Master's programs who would benefit from more stage time and technical development before beginning auditions.

Auditions Plus One of the major online sources for finding auditions in the "unamplified" singing world.

coaching A work session with a coach, analogous to a lesson with a teacher.

company Used throughout this book as shorthand for opera company.

comprimario Smaller supporting roles in operas. Typically refers to roles classified as "Secondary" or "Bit" in AGMA Schedule C.

corporation A type of business classification that (in most cases) protects its owner from personal legal and financial responsibility. This type of business pays taxes on its profits.

deductions, tax Certain business-related expenses that the Internal Revenue Service allows a person to deduct—in whole or in part—from their taxable income.

Deutsche Bühnen-Jahrbuch (DBJ) An annual publication of the German government that lists the staff and contact information of every theater, agency, and presenting organization in Germany.

domain name The top-level address for a website, for example "google.com" or "harvard.edu."

148   Glossary

donor housing   One form of artist housing utilized by performing organizations. Artists live in the private home of the company's donors.

entrepreneur   A person who creates a product or service for which there is often no extant market, and who undertakes significant financial risk to do so. An innovator. Someone who links an idea with an opportunity in the hope of reaping financial benefit.

Equity (AEA)   The labor union representing theater actors, including musical theater.

fach   A German system of vocal subclassifications created to protect singers in a Fest ensemble from being made to perform repertoire that is inappropriate for their voices. An administrative tool much more than an artistic one, despite the way it is used in the United States.

Fest   In theaters in German-speaking countries, the resident ensemble of professional singers. Singers work on annual contracts with specified roles and services, for which they receive salary and benefits. Can also be used as a verb (i.e. "to fest" is to work on a Fest contract in Germany, Austria, or Switzerland).

graduate assistant (GA)   A category of employment held by graduate students at universities whereby they typically receive some degree of tuition waiver in addition to some defined stipend for on-campus labor, typically of an academic variety (e.g. assisting the Instructor of Record in a course, teaching applied lessons, providing administrative support to a department).

GSA Per Diem Rate   The exact amount of money the United States government (via the General Services Administration) allots for travel-related expenses, calibrated based on city and month, and updated annually. Singers most frequently use this to calculate deductions for work-related travel on their taxes.

headshot   A professional shoulders- or neck-up photograph used in theater, opera, and film. Norms differ from those of more commercial portraiture, so look for photographers who have experience in your specific industry and whose work looks consistent with how you would like to be portrayed.

house   (see "company")

international house/company   Shorthand for an opera company that regularly hires artists who work at companies all over the world, and/or are based outside the United States. This is a relatively small group, and somewhat flexible.

Kloiber   The *Handbuch der Oper* is the official guide to the *fach* system in Germany. Written in German.

Lead/Featured/Secondary/Bit   Role classifications which can be found on AGMA Schedule C. Lead is largest; Bit is smallest, in terms of amount of music in a role.

League of American Orchestras (LAO)   The trade organization for American orchestras. Provides member listings, job listings, training, advocacy, and other services.

limited liability company (LLC)   A type of business classification that (in most cases) protects its owner from personal legal and financial liability. Unlike a corporation, an LLC's earnings and losses "pass-through" to the personal taxes of its owner(s).

manager   (see "Agent")

Musical America (MA)   An online and print publication that contains industry news, a massive contact database, an industry job board, artist and management news, and many other services, both for free and via subscription.

musics   A term commonly used in musicology to refer to the broad and diverse range of musical styles within a given culture.

National Opera Association (NOA)   A national (United States) organization promoting "excellence in opera education and pedagogy through its support of a diverse community of opera educators and professionals" (Source: NOA.org).

Opera America (OA)   The trade organization for administrative professionals in the opera industry. Opera America provides a wealth of valuable career information for singers on their website as well as training programs and discounted media recording throughout the year at their headquarters, the National Opera Center in New York City.

Operabase   Perhaps the most robust opera-specific database on the Internet. Provides at least a decade worth of artistic programming information for most European opera houses and a good number of companies in North and South America, among others. Also allows users to research singers, agents, and contact information for opera companies throughout the world.

Pay-to-Sing (PTS)   Shorthand for a tuition-based performance training program for singers.

per diem   (as distinct from the GSA Per Diem Rate) Money paid by a presenting organization to cover meals.

press kit   A professional document that includes a headshot, bio, and résumé.

Professional/Performer's Diploma (PD)   (see "Artist Diploma")

publicist   A professional who represents artists to press outlets and amplifies press to appropriate channels.

150 *Glossary*

regional house/company An opera company that hires singers almost exclusively from within the United States.
repertoire book A binder or book containing a singer's audition repertoire.
repertoire list A complete account of the repertoire an artist has studied and performed in a broad range of genres. Useful for graduate school auditions and academic job interviews/recitals, among other things.
Resident Artist Program (RAP) A young artist training program attached to an opera company, in which singers are paid and engaged in regular main stage roles.
résumé A one-page list of your professional experience and training.
Schedule C (AGMA) AGMA's listing of information about most of the standard opera repertory, including roles and their size/classifications (Lead/Featured/Secondary/Bit). When working at AGMA houses, these classifications correlate to minimum pay scales, but they are also helpful for negotiating purposes in non-AGMA houses. Schedule C is located under the "Membership" tab on the AGMA website but is not behind the paywall.
segregated fees At a university, these are fees (typically calculated on a per-credit basis) charged to students in addition to tuition. If you receive a graduate/teaching assistant financial package from a graduate school program, it typically includes a full tuition waiver, but may or may not include segregated fees.
Sitzprobe Typically the first rehearsal with orchestra. Singers are technically seated (the "sitz" part) but may stand when they sing. Note distinction between *Sitzprobe* and *Wandelprobe*.
sole proprietorship The simplest form of business. Refers to an entity owned and operated by a single person who is personally responsible for its debts.
teaching assistant (TA) (see "graduate assistant")
terminal degree The highest degree awarded in an academic field. In many disciplines, it is the Ph.D; in performance, the D.M.A.; in acting and theater directing, the M.F.A. Typically required in order to qualify for tenure at a major research university.
Truelinked A European job listing site for opera singers specializing in "jump-ins" for Europe-based singers at European houses. Also vets candidates for productions one or more seasons ahead of time. Truelinked purchased Operabase in 2019.
tuition waiver Part of the compensation package for graduate and teaching assistants, it is a vehicle by which a department pays tuition on a student's behalf. May be good for partial tuition remission through full tuition plus fees. See your award letter for details.

Glossary   151

union, labor   An organized group of workers, typically in similar professions, formed to protect and advocate for the rights and interests of its members.

vanity company   A type of regional opera company whose principal members tend to cast themselves in productions. A derisive term which should not be used in mixed company.

Wandelprobe   An alternative to the *Sitzprobe*; a type of orchestra rehearsal where singers are placed on the stage in a series of static positions, but do not engage in staged movement, utilize props, or wear any costume pieces (with the possible exception of costume shoes). Sometimes referred to simply as "Wandel" (pronounced in German, with an initial "v" sound).

YAP Tracker   A subscription-based job board for opera singers that lists thousands of opportunities per year. Derives its name from the acronym for Young Artist Programs.

Young Artist Program (YAP)   A type of training program for preprofessional opera singers. YAPs are paid opportunities connected to professional opera companies which provide advanced training and performance opportunities to bridge the gap between a singer's formal education and full-time main stage career.

Index

Note: Page numbers in *italic* refer to Figures; Page numbers in **bold** refer to Tables; and Page numbers in ***bold italic*** refer to boxes

A/B/C/D Houses 9, 10
abusive behaviors 51–52, 54
accompanists *see* pianists
agents 23, 78, 86
American Guild of Musical Artists (AGMA) 111
aria lists *see* repertoire lists
Artist Diploma Database 64–66
Artistic Administrators 12
artistic advisors 57–61
artistic directors 11
Assistant Stage Managers (ASMs) 137
auditions 3, 4, 115–116, 117–118, 123–126; pianists 116, 118, 119, 121, 122, *123*, 125–126, 128

biographies 77–78, 81–83, 87
Blythely Oratonio 95
Board of Directors 57–61
Boston Pops 18
budgeting 99–102, 109, 111

career advisors 57–61
coaches 58, 60, 61
commissions 24, 26, 28–29
companies databases 64
competitions 18, 19–20, 21
Concept Meetings 135
concert work 16–18, 20, 139
contacts databases 64
contracts 28–29
cover assignments 138

databases 63–67, 71
Davis, R. 82–83
designer runs 135
Directors of Artistic Administration 12
donor functions 139
dress rehearsals 136

Education Directors 12
entrepreneurship 4
Epstein, M. 57
etiquette 137–138
European Audition Database 67
Executive Directors 11
expenses 99, 102, 104

Facebook 93
fach classification system 26, 60–61
feedback 59, 61, 64, 68–69
Fellowship Database 64–66
finances 106, **107**, 108, 111–112; budgeting 99–102, 109, 111; expenses 99, 102, 104; income 99, 100–102, 104; retirement 108; student loans 108; taxes 103–106, **107**, 109
formal training 35, 36, 37–42; graduate schools 37, 38, 39–42, 80, 108; Resident Artist Programs 36, 38–39, 42, 48–49, 70; Young Artist Programs 3, 12, 19, 36, 38–39, 42, 47–48, 49–50, 53, 54, 69–71, 80, 115–116
Fry, D. S. 109–111

Index   153

General Directors 12
Graduate School Database 64–66
graduate schools 37, 38, 39–42,
    80, 108
GSA Per Diem Rate 104, 105

Harrington, J. 1–2
Harrington, M. 1
Holloway, D. 133

income 99, 100–102, 104
inner circle 57–61
input fatigue 60, 61, 69
Instagram 93–94
international companies 9, 10
international houses 10

Johnson, J. 106, 108–109

League of American Orchestras
    (LAO) 17
#LindsayPlaysUkulele 95
Liverman, W. 95

main stage work 3, 80, 116, 132, 135
managers 23–30, 58–59, 60, 61, 71
marketing 63, 71
Massie, M. 92, 93–94
Meachem, L. 92, 93
memorization 132–133
#metoo movement 51
Metropolitan Opera 50
Musical America 10
Musical Directors 11
music education 2; see also formal
    training; non-academic programs
music industry 2; see also opera
    industry
music rehearsals 136

non-academic programs 45, 46–49,
    50, 53–54; Pay-to-Sing 37–38,
    45–46, 115; Resident Artist
    Programs 36, 38–39, 42, 48–49,
    70; Tiered Young Artist Programs
    49; Tuition-Free Tuition-Based
    Programs 47; Young Artist
    Programs 3, 12, 19, 36, 38–39, 42,
    47–48, 49–50, 53, 54, 69–71, 80,
    115–116
Nytch, J. 4

ongoing training 3
online strategies 3, 90, 93–94;
    websites 81, 83–84, 90–93, 94–96
Opera America (OA) Professional
    Company Members 9
#OperaBard 96
Opera America Budget Levels 9, 10
Opera Career Breakdown 37
Opera Career Roadmap 35, 36
opera companies 9, 11–13
Opera Cowgirls 95
opera houses 9–11
opera industry 2, 9, 50, 140, 144–146;
    abusive behaviors 51–52, 54
Operapreneurship 4–5
opera singers 4–5, 20, 35, 134,
    140–141, 144–146
orchestras 16–19
orchestras programs 19

Paid Resident Artist Programs 38–39
Paid Young Artist Programs 38–39
Pay-to-Sing (PTS) 37–38, 45–46,
    115; Database 66–67
performing arts festivals 18
pianists 116, 118, 119, 121, 122,
    123, 125–126, 128
Pops Orchestras 18–19, 20–21
Press Database 67
press kits 78, 81, 83
principal artists 138–139
Production Meetings 135
Production Stage Managers
    (PSMs) 136
professional companies 3
professional conduct 3; see also
    abusive behaviors
professional documents 77–83,
    84–86, 87; biographies 77–78,
    81–83, 87; press kits 78, 81, 83;
    prospectus 85–86; repertoire lists
    78, 84–85, 116; résumés 68, 77,
    78–80, 87
professional work 35, 36
program directors 70
prospectuses 85–86
PTS see Pay-to-Sing (PTS)

radio promotions 139
recital series 18
references 79–80, 116

regional companies 9, 10
regional houses 10–11
rehearsals 135–136
rejection 127
repertoire books 118–122
repertoire lists 78, 84–85, 116, 118
research 63–68, 69–71
Resident Artist Programs (RAPs) 36, 38–39, 42, 48–49, 70
résumés 68, 77, 78–80, 87
retainers 24
retirement 108
Review Database 67
reviews 67, 83–84
Richie, A. 63
room runs 135
Rule of 25s 133

Santa Fe Opera Apprentice Singer program 48
self-assessment 67–68, 71
service providers 63
side jobs 102–103, 111
significant others 59, 61, 139–140
singers 2
sing-through rehearsals 135
Sitzprobe rehearsals 136
social media 81, 93–94, 139; websites 81, 83–84, 90–93, 94–96
spreadsheets 63–64
stage directors 11
stage managers (SMs) 136–137
staging rehearsals 135
student loans 108
Studio Managers 12
Summer Tuition-Based Training Programs (Pay-to-Sing) *see* Pay-to-Sing (PTS)

taxes 103–106, **107**, 109
teachers 2, 58, 60–61, 71
team members 57–61, 69, 71
technical ("Tech") rehearsals 136
Tier 1/2/3/4/5 Houses 9–10
Tiered Young Artist Programs 49
traditions 137–138
training programs 3, 47, 48, 53, 134; *see also* formal training; non-academic programs
tuition based programs 47, 53
Tuition-Free Tuition-Based Programs 47
TV promotions 139
Twitter 94

undergraduate degrees 37
undergraduate teachers 39, 40
underrepresented singers 52–53, 144
understudying 138

vanity companies 9–11
vanity houses *see* vanity companies
voice programs 2, 37, 39, 144

Wandelprobe rehearsals 136
websites 81, 83–84, 90–93, 94–96

YAP Database 66–67
YAP Tracker 18, 19, 115, 116, **117**
Young Artist Programs (YAPs) 3, 12, 19, 36, 38–39, 42, 47–48, 49–50, 53, 54; auditions 115–116; research 69–71; résumés 80; *see also* Pay-to-Sing (PTS)

For Product Safety Concerns and Information please contact our EU
representative GPSR@taylorandfrancis.com
Taylor & Francis Verlag GmbH, Kaufingerstraße 24, 80331 München, Germany

www.ingramcontent.com/pod-product-compliance
Lightning Source LLC
Chambersburg PA
CBHW072219240426
43670CB00038B/2196